DEDICATION

Dedicated to my Shepherd, Jesus Christ.

Dedicated to my wife, Christina.
Without her patience I could not have finished this book.

Also dedicated to those sheepdogs who protect the flock.
Stay strong. Stay safe.

TABLE OF CONTENTS

INTRODUCTION

On December 9, 2007, there was a horrific mass murder at a Colorado-based youth missions training center and the church that funded that center. On that fateful Sunday morning at Youth With a Mission and New Life Church, a man with a grudge set out to kill as many people as possible. In total, he succeeded in killing four people and wounding several.

His rampage was only stopped by a volunteer at New Life Church who happened to be on the church's security team. Because she was armed, that security person was able to defend the church and stop a mass murderer. If she and her companions weren't there, the body count would likely have been higher in this 10,000+ member mega-church.

A couple months after that incident, I approached my pastor with a simple question: Did our church have any plans or team in place to deal with a violent incident like this? When he told me that the church did not have any plans for response, I simply asked if I could put together some emergency response plans. I also asked if he would mind if I began carrying my concealed sidearm concealed to church on Sundays, starting the very next Sunday. He said I would be welcome to do so.

During the next month, I worked on plans to set up a small team to handle the safety aspects for a church with a 100,000 square-foot facility and a regular attendance of 800-900+ on Sundays. I also had to plan for the special events we hold where we may have over 2,500 people in our facility or parking lot at one time. This started as a small task and quickly grew into a more daunting plan. It seemed every time I stopped planning, it felt like God "whacked" me upside the head and simply said, "Not enough." By the time I leaned back and felt a nod that the plan was enough in His eyes, this "small task" had grown into a full-blown ministry team.

When I approached the pastor with the end "safety team" plan, he nodded, smiled, and then said, "Let's take it to the LT (the Leadership Team, the Church Board)." After I presented the plan to the church board, including plans for recruiting, funding, and even armed team members, I received overwhelming approval. As happens most often in the volunteer-driven church, I was then told to "Go for it." The only way to get it started would be for me to take on the responsibility of implementing the plan; I would become the volunteer leader of this new team. As I felt this was placed on my heart by God, I began working on building this team into a ministry.

As I began working, I quickly realized a couple things.

First, most churches do not have any type of planning or team in place for safety emergencies. Whether it is a cardiac arrest in the middle of Sunday worship, a broken arm at a youth event, or a violent attack on the church, most churches either assume someone will help or naively assume that it cannot happen in their church because it is "the Lord's House."

Those few churches that do have plans are typically the larger churches, and often they keep the existence of any team buried, as if ashamed of thinking and planning for the worst. From hidden first aid kits and automated external defibrillator (AED) devices, to a strict "no talking about the team" approach to the team itself, churches seem to want to keep any thought of "danger" out of their parishioners' minds. Even when I contacted the few churches that I knew had teams in place, they were uncooperative in the least, and even hostile for mentioning it at the worst. So I began to plan and work largely on my own.

There are several great resources out there that offer direct tactical or strategic planning for churches. With topics like landscaping, video cameras, and even how to respond to a violent incident, the vast majority of the materials pull corporate-based security concepts into the church world. The Department of Homeland Security (DHS) and the Federal Emergency Management Agency (FEMA) have even released a series of documents and videos that discuss emergency planning for houses of worship.

The largest liability in this material, in my opinion, is that it uniformly considers security from a "corporate security" point of view and, at best, attempts to stick a "ministry" label on it. Don't get me wrong: all of this material is a great resource for someone who has never looked at physical security and planning. Unfortunately, there does not seem to be any resources available that talk about building a church safety team as a MINISTRY from the ground up. There are also a lot of other considerations that nobody mentions when you are starting this type of ministry. For example, I have spent the last several years struggling with everything from a hostile staff member, to theft, to firing personnel, and even a question of whether taking water to someone was a worthwhile endeavor (that story is a doozy).

So why would I write this book? After having spent those last several years working in and on this Safety Team Ministry, after countless hours of training, and after numerous incidents of "Oh, I never even thought of that," I thought I'd write a book for those who may just be starting out or who may be early in their ministry and haven't seen some of these issues crop up yet. It is my hope that anyone can use this book, learn from my mistakes, laugh alongside my stories, and avoid the same traps and pitfalls.

Throw the Box Away!

As we get started, I want to explain one concept that I believe is incredibly important, and in fact, one that I try to live and work by. Throughout our lives, most of us have heard the expression that says we should "think outside the box." Most often, the well-intentioned person explains that many people live their lives inside a virtual "box" created by their feelings and experiences with walls carved out of their fears and beliefs. The motivational speaker will then explain that we must get over those walls and begin to think outside the box.

Unfortunately, human nature loves walls. Walls make us feel safe and secure. Those that want to step outside of those walls are taught to "think outside the box." Regrettably, when most people begin to "think outside the box", they get so concerned with making sure that they think "outside" the box that they still define their lives by that SAME BOX. Instead of worrying about the inside dimensions, they worry about the outside dimensions. Are they far enough "outside the box"? Is this idea "outside the box"? What about that one?

I would rather propose a different solution. Do NOT think outside the box. Instead, throw the stupid box away. Let me say that again: Do NOT think outside the box of your thinking; throw the box completely away. When you throw "the box" away, your fears, your doubts, and your chains all drop away. What does "no box" thinking look like? Instead of asking, "Is this idea outside the box," you should ask yourself, "How can I use this idea?" Don't be afraid to go for broke. Shoot for the stars… you might hit the moon. You might only reach orbit. At worst, the explosion will be spectacular. Either way, if you don't throw the box away, you won't ever have the chance to break free.

So what does this have to do with a Safety Team Ministry? There are chapters in this book where I am going to tell you to break tradition. I want you to be open enough to explore what a safety team might look like that functions as a real, soul-saving, God-worshipping ministry.

Organizing the Book

I'd like to give you a couple notes about how I've organized this book. In each chapter, I will discuss a different point, illustrating each with personal anecdotes from my service. In each chapter, I will also include a final sub-section called "Lessons Learned." In this sub-section, I will wrap up the illustrations and talk about what lessons you can, and should, pull from my experience, even if it is a matter of what NOT to do. Finally, at the end of each chapter, I will pose some questions for you to think about as you move forward with your ministry.

I also would like to point out that I will almost always use "church" in reference to the Safety Team Ministry. While I come from a Christian church perspective, I do not wish to exclude anyone. I believe that the vast majority of what I talk about in this book will apply to most, if not every, "house of worship" or para-church organization around. Whether church, synagogue, mosque, temple, or some other para-church ministry, the principles in this book apply to your ministry. As it happens, I come from a Christian perspective, and my language reflects that.

With that said, strap on your seatbelt, make sure your seat back and tray table is in the upright and locked position, and prepare for takeoff.

Chapter 1

THIS IS A MINISTRY

Throughout this book, I will refer to the Safety Team as the Safety Team Ministry. This is because I believe that any Safety Team that works within a church or para-church organization must be a true ministry at its very heart. You might think this a no-brainer, "Of course it's a ministry. It's something that the church does. By definition this is a ministry."

Well, I include this chapter because a fair number of the safety or security teams that I see in churches do not approach the job from a servant's heart. Serving on the team is often seen as a "security" job, and while I believe security to be necessary, it is not treated as a ministry service to the congregation. Those who create a safety team for their church do not intend to separate the team from actually serving in ministry, but the nature of the job and training can easily shift focus away from serving the congregation to "protecting" or "guarding" the congregation. And while part of the job may include those functions, a true Safety Team Ministry must serve the church and those who attend.

Based on the Latin word for service (ministerium), any

Safety Team Ministry must be first and foremost viewed as a ministry and service for the church. Most secular security teams concentrate on "security" instead of service. Whether they are simply keeping inventory control or handling basic first aid-type issues, a security team is hired to do one thing: secure the premises and those inside. In the church, however, those who serve on the team must see themselves as servants within the church, serving and caring for those who are on campus, even those who might want to harm the church or its people.

It is this attitude shift that will have the greatest impact on the church where the Safety Team ministers. Instead of being seen simply as security, any Safety Team must be seen as a ministry. And to be seen that way requires the Safety Team to act as a ministry. This attitude shift has to extend from the top down and must permeate the entire culture of the Safety Team Ministry.

This all starts at the head of the team. Whoever is leading the team, whether volunteer or paid staff, must have the heart of a servant to be a true leader. Their passion must be towards serving and helping, not power or authority. When I first started the Safety Team at Frontline Community Church in Grand Rapids, Michigan, I will admit that I did not have the right attitude. I was more concerned with security rather than service. I will later talk about how this affected my volunteer recruiting in another chapter, but this philosophy really skewed my team, and it has taken a complete rework, and the loss of several very valuable volunteers before the ministry began serving as it should.

Even though I promoted the team as the "Safety Team," I now realize that this was merely lip service to allay concerns about having so-called security around. Even though I had made some honest early attempts, my methodology was flawed. I had a heart to help keep the church safe, but, unfortunately, I chose the wrong method. My attitude was "security first," and this permeated my training and the attitudes of my team. This attitude caused friction with several members of the congregation and even some of the staff. It also caused friction among our team's members.

Then one spring, an incident happened that sparked a chain-reaction, forever changing how I would approach the team and even how the team would be composed. I asked for approval to add another member to my "Special Safety" team, the portion of my team that is armed while on duty. As this approval proceeded through the executive staff (senior pastor and executive pastor), I was met with a great deal of resistance. The more I questioned, the more resistance I encountered. This became a vicious cycle that eventually triggered a full review of not only the Safety Team as a whole but also of my leadership specifically.

At the time, I could not understand what was happening or why the team was meeting such resistance. As puzzled as I was, I also felt angry; it felt like I was being attacked personally by the executive pastor. I knew that we had a fundamental difference of opinion about the need for a Safety Team and especially about the need for some of our members to be armed with concealed handguns while serving. What I could not understand was his view of the "culture" of the team, or what we thought we were doing wrong.

At my lowest point, I considered resigning from my position. Several team members resigned from the Safety Team and a few even left the church, and as the summer wrapped up, I had composed my resignation letter and prepared to give it to the pastor. The only thing that was stopping me was the knowledge that, if I left, the team would quickly disintegrate and that several of the team members were upset enough to contemplate leaving the church as well. Between the actions of the executive pastor and the burden of knowing what would happen if I left, I was carrying a large weight around. It was only then that I finally did what I should have done long before... I dropped to my knees and started praying for answers.

Culture Shift

Throughout this process, I was seeking out the council of board members and other interested parties, and my eyes were opened to some of the issues that were cropping up. From the feedback they provided, I was able to look through the eyes of those outside the team and realized that my team was not following a culture of service but had become a culture that resembled mall security guards or even bouncers. From those I recruited, to our actions and training, this "security" culture was constantly reinforced and promoted. It was negatively affecting the team and having a large negative impact on the congregation.

Through prayer and the council of some trusted advisors, I was finally able to see what the team had become. At that point, I had a decision to make. I could give up, resign, and leave the church that my family had called home for 10 years. My other option was to step up in leadership, make broad changes, and change the very culture of the team. This would positively impact the team, the staff and the entire congregation as we moved forward. I spent a great deal more time in prayer trying to figure out if I was still called to do this ministry.

As I prayed to God and sought council about my decisions, I came to believe that I was already in the church that I was called to serve in... I just needed to actually start serving. With this decision came a renewed attitude of service. I started by proactively beginning to change the culture and daily operations of the team. I started focusing training on service and warmth instead of threats and security. I began to go through the remaining team members and started working with them. If they could not be re-trained to portray the right attitude, I helped them find another ministry where they could serve. I also started working with the staff more. I became more proactive in, and worked more with, their various ministry needs.

Over the next few months, the changes in the culture of the team were noticed by the staff and by the congregation. When the review process ended, I met with the senior and executive pastors, who had together prepared a list of recommendations for changes to the safety team. I actually had two lists prepared for the meeting: a list of changes that I had already implemented and a list of changes that were simply waiting on approval of the senior pastor to implement. When we compared the lists, we found out that I had already implemented a number of the recommended changes. We agreed that where the lists did not overlap were insignificant points, and we were able to work together to draw a compromise from both sides.

The culture of the team was changed. It did not happen overnight, but the changes came. We are currently a Safety Team Ministry that has regained a large amount of the respect that we lost, not just for the job we do, but for the service and ministry that we provide to the church. Over time, the changes have become so evident that I've been complimented several times by staff for the service we give, and the pastor that I clashed with so regularly has noticed the change in culture and has commended us on the shift.

It is this ministry and service model that has also granted us more leeway when the inevitable human errors have occurred. At a large event during the summer of 2012, one of my temporary event team members was gruff in handling a situation that was also compounded with some miscommunications about policies. I was able to talk to the person who was legitimately offended that following Sunday and offer apologies both personally and from the team. Because of our reputation, we were able to heal any hurt feelings, and I was able to make a report to the pastoral staff about the incident and its conclusion.

Lessons Learned

So what does a service ministry look like, and how does that compare to simply being safety or security? The largest difference is in attitude towards the congregation. Instead of walking around looking aloof, the team will smile and engage in conversation with others. Instead of standing as "guard" to the church or children's area, they will smile and welcome visitors warmly. The biggest difference is warmth and genuine smiles. Even when the Safety Team has to look out for trouble, they should be smiling and engaging. If they have to turn someone away from an area, it should be with a gentle word and a smile. To put it simply, they have to have a heart for serving people. If they have a heart for serving, they can be trained to watch for trouble.

It is incredibly important to begin your Safety Team as a ministry from the ground up. By beginning with a servant-heart outlook, your Safety Team Ministry will serve the church well. If you instead begin with a corporate security mindset, and try to patch it with a "ministry" label, your team and your church will both experience the negative effects.

- What if you started with a right heart, but wrong methods, like I did? I would advise you to do a couple things:

- Hit your knees and seek God's face for your ministry. Seeking God's will and calling MUST be your place to start.
- Find a couple advisors in your church that you can trust. They need to be outside your team so that they will give you a very different perspective. Then listen to what they have to say.
- If there are suggestions that are worthwhile, implement them immediately.
- Contact your current boss in the church as well as any of the executive staff that needs to be involved. Get any issues or complaints out in the open. This will be hard, and you will have to swallow your pride as the issues are brought to light. Pride will stand in your way. Don't let it.
- Be humble, open, and honest with your church staff. Work with the staff to work through the issues.
- Be humble, open, and honest with your team. Explain WHY any changes are necessary, and enlist their help in this ministry.

The Safety Team Ministry at our church is now an intentional service-oriented ministry. It must be treated as such, and the team has to intentionally serve the congregation.

I encourage you to take an honest look at your safety team and ask yourself the following questions:

1. Is our team a "safety team" or a "security team"?
2. Are we a ministry, or simply "hired contractors"?
3. What is the culture of our team?

Notes:

Chapter 2

WHAT'S IN A NAME?

I mentioned that the Safety Team must be more than a simple team; they must be a ministry. One of the paradigm shifts that must occur to push the team towards ministry is how they are presented to the church. One of the most effective ways of doing this is to choose the name of the team wisely.

When I first started planning and building this team, I really did not think through some of these issues. The original concept name of my team was "Emergency Response Team," or "ERT" for short. As I began planning, I began to realize that we needed a softer name for the congregation. With anything involving security, especially anything potentially involving weapons, a softer, nicer sounding name will create a different impression to the public.

When most people think of security, they think of the white or blue polyester uniform with a shiny badge.

I bet that most Americans would picture some gruff "old geezer" in a guard shack or some young "wannabe police officer" who is a bit overzealous guarding their local mall or shopping center. Having worked as a manager for a large physical security firm in Indianapolis, Indiana, I would say that the vast majority of the 400+ officers working there fell into those categories. But this is NOT the impression that any church can afford to give—God's church is supposed to welcome the hurting and broken, not intimidate or threaten them. In my opinion, churches should never have security guards because doing so shows a cognitive disconnect between the mission of the church and the practice of the church.

This perception based on language is the reason that many local law enforcement departments around the country are shifting from being called "Police" to "Public Safety". If you look around your area, you will quickly see local law enforcement that has "Public Safety" instead of "Police" on their vehicles and uniforms. It is the same reason that older generation officers might still refer to themselves as "peace officers" instead of police or law enforcement. Being a peace officer from a Public Safety Department sounds much nicer than saying that you are a law enforcement officer from the Police Department. It is all about public perception. And in public perception, EVERY word matters.

The Power of a Name

Beyond public perception, the internal perception

that is based on language is an even more integral part of the issue. With consistent reinforcement, and constant dialogue, a change to being a peace officer from a Public Safety Department will create an internal atmosphere that is different than being a "cop" from the local PD. When this internal shift corresponds to the external perception of the public, then the culture of the department shifts, and the citizens begin to notice it.

This is why we made the shift, internally and externally, to being the "Frontline Safety Team." After making the shift, I spent several months correcting anyone who asked, including pastors, staff, or congregants. It was several Sundays in a row where I was asked by the senior pastor, or the intergenerational pastor, "Hey, Bryan. Are you on security today?"

I was always quick to smile and reply, "Nope. I don't work security. I help with safety." As the staff got used to the new lingo, they, too, began using it publicly. We work hard to make sure that every communication about or from the Safety Team reads "Safety" and not "Security." In fact, one of the biggest changes was to our building use forms (and related email confirmations) that were utilized when someone reserved part of the building.

Because we have a large facility, we often have groups inside and outside the church ask to rent some portion of our facility. When we were starting the team, the Trustees thought it would be a good idea to have someone from the Safety Team present with larger groups, especially if they were not part of the church. Depending on the circumstances, this duty may even draw a small stipend for working the event. The early confirmation emails listed "Security" as a line-item, regarding times and billing. I worked with the church office for quite a while to get them to change the terminology to "Safety." After a couple meetings, and some frustration on the office administrator's part, I was able to help them understand WHY the switch was important, and more importantly, how much it would cut down their questions and concerns.

They had received several calls and questions regarding whether "security" was necessary for events, especially with events that were held by long-time church members. While there had been some actual damage and theft which would have warranted the presence, the real threat level was very low for "security" needs. When approached about this from the church's office administrator, I explained how she could cut the vast majority of those calls out completely. If she simply changed the word security to the word safety, she would receive far fewer calls. For those few calls she received, I gave her an additional strategy: she should let the caller know that the Safety Team is there in case anything goes wrong. With trained and certified Professional Responder-level emergency personnel on hand, if anything does happen, they, or their guests, will be safe and protected.

After she made the changes to the forms, the number of calls she received dropped dramatically. For those who did call to inquire about the safety line item, she was able to give them an explanation that satisfied them, without causing additional alarm or offense.

This is the same answer that I give almost anyone who asks what I do at the church. I tell them, as leader of the Safety Team, we are there to respond to any emergencies that come up, especially medical-related emergencies. With our training and equipment, we can respond to virtually any medical crisis professionally, as we wait for the ambulance crews to arrive. When couched in those terms, people are usually very pleased that a Safety Team is present.

This change to "Safety Team" had one other huge benefit. As I mentioned in the prior chapter, our outer appearance and branding was "safety" but our actions shouted "security," even to those who we were supposed to be serving. While we went through the tumult and trouble of revamping the ministry, one of the things that I was made aware of was this "security" attitude. At times, our team was frankly more of a hindrance than a service in the ministry of the church. After the dust had settled, I realized what being a "Safety Team Ministry" meant to the church, and to our group.

As silly as it sounds, words have meaning. By making the switch in all of our verbal and written communication, we can internalize that function of the ministry. Instead of being "security," we became "safety." By accepting on the inside the very verbiage that we were using on the outside, our very culture shifted from "mall cop" to "safety." Although we still train vigorously for security issues, our language and internal thinking shifted to reflect an ideal of safety. At that point, we no longer acted like security guards or bouncers.

Lessons Learned

As I train other churches, I always recommend that they adopt the "Safety Team" language. In fact, I'm very quick to correct the verbiage in any training session or when meeting with church staff or leadership. I actually look forward to the first time that someone starts talking about "security," especially when it relates to what I do at my church. I use that moment to correct the verbiage and reshape the culture of the church volunteer team. Once I explain why I'm so adamant about using the correct terminology, the staff and leadership most often understand and agree.

The language that you use, internally and externally, will affect the very culture of your team. Remember, words have profound meaning. Language and training go hand in hand. Begin to switch your verbiage. Encourage your team to change their language as well. Begin to quickly, politely, and with a disarming smile, correct ANY usage of bad terminology. If your senior pastor asks you about "security," smile and let them know that your team doesn't "work security." Instead, you "help with safety."

This is where you should begin to examine your training as well. How much time do you spend on corporate security concepts? While those security concepts and awareness are important, train your team to serve with a servant's heart. Structure your policies to reflect those changes. In short, let the verbiage that you SHOULD be using help you become the Safety Team Ministry that you can be.

As you start, join, or revamp your church Safety Team, remember, the language that we use invokes certain images and feelings.

Consider the following questions:

1. What language are you using? Does it invoke images of "mall cops?" Or does it, instead, convey a sense of ministry and helping others?

2. What does the name of your team communicate to those that you serve?

3. How can you change your training to reflect "Ministry" more?

Notes:

Chapter 3

WHERE DO YOU FIT?

The title of this chapter is a play on words that applies to the church where I serve: Frontline Community Church. Those who serve as greeters, ushers, and the parking lot welcome team are part of the F.I.T. Team, the First Impressions Team. This ministry is where visitors and members alike form their first impression of the church every Sunday morning. Until recently, the Safety Team Ministry was NOT a part of this team; instead, it was a part of the Facilities team, and managed by the Facilities Manager.

The vast majority of churches who have a Safety Team place their team under the facilities staff person. This seems to be a logical place to put a security-based team because security teams in the corporate/secular world tend to fall under asset management or facilities. In most cases, church-based safety or security teams are placed here for one of three reasons: 1) the person who helps initiate the team comes from a corporate security background; 2) the executive pastoral staff does not know where to place the team; or 3) the staff follows the lead of churches around them and places the team under the facilities staff.

At first glance, the facilities staff might seem to be the logical manager for this type of team. Safety and security teams often have facility safety as part of their duties, and the personnel often roam the back halls and unused areas of the church to check for unusual or troubling activity. Safety and security teams also work extensively with other ministries in the church, and the only other department that really works with as many other ministries is the facilities staff.

Change Your Thinking

I believe that this is an area where you should completely throw the box away regarding what is "normal" for Safety Teams. Instead, I recommend a different way of looking at this: any safety/security team should become a part of the same ministry that includes greeters and ushers. I believe that this arrangement can have a several advantages over the traditional placement of the Safety Team. By placing your Safety Team under the same umbrella as the greeters and ushers, the team is treated as a ministry, able to help keep offerings safe, and able to work with other team members who can help in times of emergency.

Perhaps the most important reason for having the Safety Team work with this other ministry directly reinforces the "ministry" aspect of the team. As I talked about in the first chapter, your safety team MUST be a ministry from the start. By being a part of a ministry that is, by definition, staffed with friendly and welcoming people, you help the culture of the safety team become one that will exemplify the very characteristics they need to have. Remember, if they are trained to serve and are surrounded by people who are serving, the team will have a culture of serving.

When the team is serving with the ushers and greeters, they are also naturally better able to help protect and watch over the offering as it is being collected. During the last couple years, the United States of America have seen a surge in very brazen robberies in which the Sunday offerings are stolen during services. While only a small fraction of churches will be robbed like this, I challenge you to think about what the loss of one Sunday's offerings would do to the finances of your local church. Having an overt Safety Team involved in the collection becomes a deterrent to this type of theft.

Having safety present also helps deter another, far more common and devastating type of theft: embezzlement. It is sad that the largest losses for churches over the last several years have been from internal theft or embezzlement. The most common source of embezzlement comes from a single person who is in charge of counting the money. They will often start out justifying their actions as, "I only need this little bit to pay this bill. I'll pay it back next week." Then, while they are counting the following week's offerings, they justify a little more, "I can't pay back that, but I still need to pay this new bill." Before long, that "little" bit of money totals thousands of dollars. While I advocate that safety personnel should NEVER physically touch the money, having them present will help provide accountability for everyone involved.

The last reason for the safety team to serve in this capacity is that those greeters and ushers will often be the first responders to medical or fire/weather related emergencies. By being one staff, and doing minimal cross-training, those greeters and ushers can provide a huge help in case of emergency. This minimal cross-training can turn what could be a royal mess into a well-orchestrated response to an emergency, thus enhancing the safety of everyone concerned.

If the safety team is part of this greeting team, what should they be doing on Sunday morning? The answer is quite simple: they should be acting as greeters and cheerily welcoming folks into the church. I do not allow my team to stand in the back or off to the side and simply glower with their arms folded. One of the tremendous changes that came from our re-design was to bring the safety team to the forefront on Sunday mornings. My team is trained to mingle with the crowds in the lobby, opening doors and greeting people. Basically, my team has become a new, additional team of greeters and welcome staff, except that we have additional training and duties. The added benefit to this is that our presence, while friendly and inviting, is still a presence. Most of the "bad guys" that might desire to do bad things will be deterred by the mere presence of the safety team.

Changing Course

When I first began putting this team together, our team was placed under the Facilities Manager, the paid staffer that was my manager. In fact, not only was the Facilities Manager my boss, but I also dual-reported directly to the head Trustee. While I got along with, and had the support of, each of my managers, this occasionally led to difficulties when I received direction from one that directly contradicted the other. To make matters even more complicated, I also directly reported to the senior pastor on any matter that involved our Special Safety Team (the part of my team that was armed). I should not have to explain how crazy and chaotic this made my job.

During the complete redesign of the team, one of the things that changed was my direct reporting and accountability. My direct reporting and accountability was shifted to the Facilities Manager only. As he became my direct manager, my path and responsibilities became clearer. The Facilities Manager and I have a great working relationship, and he trusts that I know my job and that I have the heart to serve the church. After he visited a couple of my training sessions, he now understands both how and what I teach my team. Because he knows what my team is trained to do, and he trusts me to work with them, he doesn't have to "babysit" or deal with problems from my team much, if at all.

When I began the process of writing this book, I began to think about the roles that my team plays and evaluate where they should be. As I did, I approached three key staff members to talk about where I saw the Safety Team Ministry heading. First, I broached my concerns to the Facilities Manager. I talked to him about how the team really should fall under the F.I.T. team (First Impressions Team), Frontline's greeters, ushers, and welcome team. Reluctantly, he came to agree with some of my assessments. At this point, I began to approach the Worship Arts Director. She has the dual duty of leading the worship and creative arts ministries, as well as leading the F.I.T. team.

To say she was less-than-thrilled about taking on yet another team to manage would be understating it heavily. As we talked further, I went on to assure her that my management style is to basically relieve the burden of managing my team from my boss. It is always my goal to be able to be a strong enough leader, and a good enough trainer, that my team is not a burden on my boss. As I told her, it is my job to deal with the team under me, and to take the heat for the team from the staff. Basically, I am the conduit and filter to protect both the team and my boss. In time, she began to see my point of view, and why I believed that the Safety Team should be reporting under the F.I.T. team. I have worked with her enough that she knows where my heart is, and she agrees that, on the surface, my team and the F.I.T. team do the same basic thing: greet people warmly.

My next step was to pitch my idea, to plant the seed, in the mind of my senior pastor, as he had the power to make the change in the organization. Once the seed was planted, I recommended the change at opportune times. As a result, he began discussing it with both the Facilities Manager and the Worship Arts Director. This is still a work in progress; this transition will slowly take place as a few more structural changes at the church need to be made.

As I write this book, I unfortunately report to two different staff members again. Thankfully, this will only last until we transition to the F.I.T. team. Until then, I report to and am accountable to the Worship Arts Director on Sunday mornings. At all other times, I report to and am accountable to the Facilities Manager. The long-term goal is to move the Safety Team reporting from facilities to the F.I.T. team, where I believe it should be. In the interim, we still warmly greet people on Sunday mornings, no matter who my current boss is.

Lessons Learned

Whether you are just starting your church's Safety Team, or you are leading an existing team, where do you fit in the church? Does your team work as part of the Facilities staff, or is it front-and-center for welcoming people to your church alongside your greeters? The benefits of your team becoming part of your church's welcoming greeters far outweigh any disadvantages.

With a warm, visible presence, your Safety Team will be a ministry that "FITs" in the church. By warmly greeting people to your church, you act as an ambassador for your church and serve as a deterrent in case any "bad guys" have decided to visit your church. By being available for offerings/giving time, you can prevent theft and/or embezzlement.

You WILL face resistance if you recommend that the Safety Team Ministry be placed on the same team as the greeters and ushers. This breaks all of the current conventions, especially for those who come from a corporate security background. Throw the box away, and help your leadership do the same. Keep your Safety Team as a ministry. By working with, and among, your greeters and ushers, your Safety Team Ministry can serve with warmth and caring, while helping protect the church and her ministries.

I had the privilege recently to train a smaller church's safety team that was just starting up. The head of that Safety Team was one of my original team members and had assumed similar duties at his new church home. In that training and setup, I was glad to see that he had remembered what we had gone through. He had convinced his pastor and board to allow him to create this new safety team as a new part of the existing greeter and usher structure. While I worked with him, I realized that he "got it." He understands this new role for safety.

Do you?

Here are a couple questions to think about:

1. Where does your safety team fit in your church?

2. Does this embrace the mission of ministry, or does it minimize the ministry in favor of the job?

3. If not, where SHOULD they fit? Under which ministry should your Safety Team be serving?

Notes:

Chapter 4

HIRE FOR PERSONALITY
TRAIN FOR COMPETENCE

Now that you've figured out that you have an actual ministry, have started by calling it the "right" name, and have found a great place in your church's structure, let's talk about WHO you are going to hire and HOW you are going to train them.

At this stage, either you are starting from scratch and will need to recruit your team, or you already have a team in place and need to evaluate those team members. If you do not already have a team in place, you are probably trying to figure out how to fill your ranks with the warm bodies necessary for any volunteer service/ministry. Most churches and ministries are in such dire need of volunteers that they will take anyone who comes to them. We have a tendency to rubber stamp anyone that comes along, often rationalizing that they wouldn't be there serving if they weren't called by God to do so. And if you do have a team already in place, chances are there are a few "warm bodies" that are filling up slots in your group.

Hiring the Right Person(ality)

For most ministries, finding warm bodies can be seen as "acceptable." While not ideal, the fact that someone has volunteered is more than enough to overlook any warning signs or cues that a volunteer is in the wrong ministry. I would caution that this is absolutely the worst approach to recruiting and building a Safety Team Ministry. Instead, you must hire for personality and willingness to learn. Someone who has the right personality and is willing to learn can be trained for competence and performance.

A quick note here: You have to view this process as if you are actually "hiring" someone for the position, even if it is an unpaid volunteer position. If you choose to look at your team as simply "church volunteers," you will end up missing the point. Your team is one that has been given a lot of trust and authority in the church, sometimes grudgingly. A safety team is charged with keeping the people on the church campus safe. And if your team is one that has permission to be armed, an even greater trust has been given to you, and usually even more grudgingly. You cannot afford to treat your team as typical volunteers—they are your team, and that means that they must have your trust. You need to create a specific "job description," recruit them, and "hire" them with all the care shown when recruiting for a high-paying executive position.

Why is it more important to hire someone for personality than for experience? Well, if you hire for experience, you may be stuck with the wrong personality. If you hire for personality, you can train for experience, and it is far easier to train someone for experience than to get them to change their personality. Remember where you are supposed to "fit" in. As a team that is front and center during Sunday mornings, they will be greeting people as they come through the doors. Your team must have a smile on their face, a warm personality, and be willing to engage with all kinds of people in a friendly, caring, non-threatening manner.

There are only two mandatory qualifications to this rule of hiring for personality. First, all of your team must have a clean background to be able to work with children and students. In the age of the adult predator scandal and global news, a clean record is absolutely a requirement for any church volunteers who work with kids or students. Also, any members that might be on an armed Safety Team need to have experience and competence already. They cannot "learn on the job." An armed team member must be trained and proficient with their firearm before they ever sign in for duty. Please understand: none of this negates having the "right" personality. In fact, you will find that the toughest part of staffing your team will be finding those who fit the personality and who possess any enhanced qualifications that you need.

By hiring for the right personality, you will be able to avoid issues and personnel conflicts that might crop up otherwise. When I first launched the Safety Team Ministry at Frontline, I was in the "warm body" mode of hiring. Anyone who wanted to join did so. I went through training with each member, and as they came on board, they cycled into service. I had one gentleman that was a very jovial person. He was normally just a good-natured, light-hearted person, but when he was on duty, especially when he put on our team polo, his demeanor changed. He transformed from greeter to bouncer, with his smiles and gentle laughter giving way to scowls and seriousness. For some reason, a certain percentage of the population will always make a "hardline" change when they are wearing any sort of a "uniform," especially in a "security" or law enforcement situation.

As will often happen in these cases, his demeanor caused several church members to complain to the senior pastor. Unfortunately, I was too myopic to see the behavior changes and was not able to recognize the situation on my own. Once the behaviors were pointed out to me, I could see his change in demeanor and even watched it happen in the course of a regular Sunday service. I began working with him extensively, but it seemed that he just could not get out of that "bouncer" mode when on duty. This went on for several weeks as I tried desperately to help him correct course. Unfortunately, I finally had to fire him from the team.

How did I fire him? The first thing I did was try to assess EXACTLY what the problem was, and how it could possibly be avoided. As I mentioned above, there is a certain percentage of people who are just hard-wired to react that way. Once I was able to pinpoint the primary cause, I then began looking at the other ministries in the church to see where I thought he might fit in. Even though I could no longer have him on my team, I did not want to just cut him loose. Underneath the demeanor change, he really did have a servant's heart, and he was sincere about serving in the church. Once I found a ministry that I thought would work for him, I directly approached the head of that ministry to talk about the shift.

None of this was done with an attempt to spread rumors or talk behind my friend's back. In fact, it was basically the opposite. When I approached this other volunteer leader, I explained what was going on with this volunteer, and, more importantly, why it was happening. I then asked him if he would consider talking to my team member about serving on this other ministry. When I explained WHY I thought he might be a good fit for this other ministry, he was open to talking with my team member. Once I had found a potential new service opportunity for this volunteer, I took him out to get coffee at a local coffee shop. This was a relaxed, neutral location on purpose, as I didn't want to appear heavy handed. I wanted him to be comfortable enough to be open with me.

When I started talking to this volunteer, I was absolutely honest with him. I had been working with him for some time on these specific issues, and he knew that he was not keeping up. I was especially diligent to de-emphasize the negatives, while praising the positives that I saw in him. Towards the end, I recommended that he talk to the other ministry head and advised him that I had already broached the subject.

We were able to part from that table as friends. Because my friend enjoyed serving on the Safety Team, he was disappointed about being "fired" from the team and spent some time in the natural grieving process. After some time, this team member approached the other ministry and spent time talking with the other ministry leader. After having his questions answered, he did volunteer for this other ministry. He fit in perfectly well in the ministry and happily served there for a long time.

As an ultimate success for this story, this team member worked really hard to retrain his demeanor and body language. After some time, he requested another meeting with me. As we talked, he expressed how he wanted to have one more shot at the Safety Team Ministry. I had noticed the progress he made. With his attitude shift and demeanor shift I believed that he had been making earnest progress. As a follower of a God who believes in second chances, I could not afford to offer otherwise. In short, that volunteer rejoined the Safety Team, and worked out well until he and his wife moved to another church where she could pastor.

If your new recruit has an engaging personality, they also must be willing to learn from any training given and follow policies and procedures. They will need to be open and learn all of the aspects of the ministry. From meeting and greeting people to offering first aid during an emergency, and even watching and protecting the people of the church, your volunteers have a lot of responsibility. There is a lot of training that must happen; policies have to be followed, and your team members must learn those lessons. The sensitive nature of a Safety Team at a church mandates that they be able to kindly and courteously do their duties every time. Unfortunately, one or two major mistakes can bring a whole program down if the right people complain about your team to the senior pastor or board. And if one of those problems happens to a church staff member or board member, your ministry may end very quickly.

Every year, Frontline Community Church hosts an event called "Rockin' From the Roof." During this event, we host live Christian bands on the roof of our church and turn our parking lot into a small carnival. As a service to the area, we always give away several tons of free clothing and food to those in the community who need it. In 2012, we hosted over 3,000 people in our parking lot, giving away more than 12 tons of clothing and feeding more than 300 families with several weeks' worth of groceries. Because this is such a huge event, I have the entire team present, as well as having several "special event" safety team members present. As this is an event that is primarily for the public outside of those that call our church home, how the team acts is vitally important to the church and the ministry.

During the 2012 event, we had a couple of incidents that

were caused by or involved my team members. One of those incidents I will be addressing later, but there was one that directly pertains to this chapter. During the event setup, I assigned team members to several key areas for a stationary post. I had a couple team members that roved around, relieving those who were posted, so they could move, get out of the sun, or even get something to eat. One of these vital posts was near the clothing give-away area.

One of the "special event" team members was posted in this area alongside one of my regular team members. While I tried to be clear about duties and expectations of the day, and especially for that post, this special event member kept wandering away from his post. As he or she wandered away, we had less coverage in a high-traffic area, and this ended up causing an issue when we had a "lost mommy" incident in that area. While the Safety Team was trying to find the mother of a lost little child, a tense situation developed in the free clothing area. (Apparently, there were a couple individuals who began arguing heatedly over some clothing items.)

My regular team member was busy helping find the child's mother, and my special event member had wandered away again. As word of the argument spread, we had to respond quickly to an area, and almost had a physical altercation mar the day's events. I was eventually able to assign one of the "rovers" to the area as backup and went to go look for my lost team member. After I found the wandering team member, I realized that he was serving in the wrong ministry. He had the heart and personality, but did not have the willingness to learn and follow directions as we needed him to. Like the other team member, I was able to gently redirect him to a ministry where he fit better.

The Right Training

So what about training? What does your safety team need in their training to accomplish their duties? Even assuming that your Safety Team is a true ministry opportunity and works on and with the greeters, your team will have a secondary mission: to keep the church safe and secure. This "secondary" role of safety and security will require specialized training.

Before you can determine what your team needs for training, you will need to decide several things. First, what is the primary concern of the "security" role of your team? Where are they needed? If you do have real, substantiated security concerns, then that might be primary on your list. If your church is like most others, your primary duty will be a combination of first aid response and responding to your children's ministry. Your training emphasis will shift drastically depending on your concerns and roles.

Next, what are the rest of your team's duties? If your team is like mine, the duties might be first aid response, finding lost children, patrolling the building during services, watching for possible security threats, and even watching or escorting the offering. All of these duties need policies and training. It turns out fairly simple on paper... whatever your Safety Team Ministry has to do is what they need for both a policy and training. Also keep in mind that what they have policies and training to do, they will also need the appropriate equipment (I'll discuss this in a future chapter).

So what kind of training do they need? One of the first trainings on the list should be First Aid, Cardiopulmonary resuscitation (CPR), and, if appropriate, Automated Electronic Defibrillator (AED) training. Your team should all be certified in First Aid, CPR, and AED use. This should be an easy "sell" to the staff, as it directly impacts the safety of the congregation. If possible, I recommend that you have your team certified at the Red Cross "Professional Responder" level or at its equivalent. Although the cost can be significantly higher, the training and abilities gained are worth far more than the cost of the training itself.

Subsequent training should focus on the policies and duties of your team's job. Almost all of the duties mentioned above fall in one of two categories for training purposes: personal attitude or practical action. For personal attitude, your training should cover the basic attitudes required while working. Such attitudes as friendliness, openness, and warmth should be stressed here. Remember, your team's goal is to warmly meet and greet those who enter your doors. Attitude and bearing make all the difference between being a "bouncer" and being a representative of your God. If your team can get personal attitude right, the number of problems that they might encounter, or cause, will approach zero quickly.

Practical action training can, and will, encompass several different duties. Such training should include basic security topics of observation and awareness. By being aware, your team has the potential to spot trouble before it starts. From subtle cues in body language to clothing and packages, a state of awareness will help keep your church and your team safe. This training can help your team elevate their own awareness and understand the physiological changes that heightened stress and activity cause. By training your team to be observant, they will be able to truly see incidents as they occur. They will then be able to process the information quickly, allowing them to select the appropriate response. Observational training will allow your team to discern those things that might pique their awareness and will help them determine if there is any need for action.

Practical action training also will include responding to fire or inclement weather as well as active violence or other threats. By planning and training ahead of time, your team will know how to respond. They will be the only calm in the middle of the storm, and they'll be able to help the congregation through any incident that does arise. Such training might even include law enforcement or other first responders. Not only does this familiarize your church and team to those responders, but they can provide valuable insight to your team.

Lessons Learned

Understanding WHO you hire for your team is one of

the most important ways that you can help set your team up for success. Ignoring the personality and merely hiring for warm bodies is one of the fastest ways to set your team up for failure. In the practice of finding the right personality, you will need to learn, take in, and model the best practices of hiring managers in the corporate world.

If you want to avoid some of the heartaches that I went through, create a job description for each position on your team. Describe in it exactly who you're looking for, discussing personality and qualifications. Also describe their duties while working (on and off-duty) for the Safety Team. In short, describe your perfect candidate. Then, when you recruit prospective new team members, you will have a great tool to help determine if they will fit in your team.

You will also need to be open and willing to look at your team from outside perspectives. One of the biggest helps to me has been an "advisory team" specifically made up of a couple trusted people in the congregation who are outside of the Safety Team. My advisory team has been charged with watching the Safety Team and letting me know of any issues that they see, no matter how big or small. This team has alerted me to issues that I was able to head off more than once, allowing us to correct our issues and serve the congregation.

While you are working with your team, you will need to be able to "fire" someone. There is a philosophy that I picked up in the corporate world that describes issues with staff that I feel is very appropriate. Simply put, problems are either a "training issue" or a "personnel issue." If the problem is a training issue, then it is your job to retrain the staff member in question. This should be your first assumption in the vast majority of cases. Barring a serious act that demands firing, your first attempt should be to retrain the staff person. As a follower of a merciful Savior, it is only right that we try to help and correct volunteers. If the retraining doesn't work, or the problem is egregious enough from the start, then it is a "personnel issue." When you have a personnel issue, the only solution is to move them out of your ministry. As I have previously stated, this should be done with dignity and grace, helping the volunteer find a better ministry to serve in when possible.

When you have the team that you need, you will then need to develop a plan to train your team to be able to fulfill the required duties. If you cannot train your team, contact someone who can. When training your team, keep in mind their primary goal is service, and their important secondary goal is safety/security. Train for their experience, and train them into excellence.

In the end, your best team will come from hiring for personality and willingness to learn, and then training that team for competence in their job. Is this your policy?

A few questions to answer:

1. Are you "recruiting and hiring" or are you just taking any warm body?

2. Are you hiring warm bodies or are you hiring for personality?

3. What can you do to recruit and hire the right personalities?

4. Are there any "warm bodies" on your current team that need to be replaced?

Notes:

Make a list of potential new team members:

(Now contact them)

Chapter 5

WORKING WITH OTHER MINISTRIES

If the safety team at any church is doing their job, they will end up working with nearly every ministry in the church in some way. Some ministries will require a great deal of coordination and cooperation, while others will not be so taxing. From the senior pastor on down to facilities and office administration, and everywhere in between, the safety team is/should be one of the few truly cross-church ministries within the building. My goal is to help you avoid some of the pitfalls that I've dealt with, as well as help you deal with staff and ministries while avoiding ministry clashes.

How well you work with the pastoral staff and the other ministries of your church will generally be based upon two large categories that only YOU can control: how well you treat other people and ministries and your personal credibility and leadership ability. If you do not treat others

45

exceedingly well, you will not be able to work with or around those staff and ministry volunteers that you offend. This often is accomplished by maintaining the highest level of professionalism when dealing with the inevitable problems, incidents, and conflicts. The other part of this component is your personal credibility and leadership. WHO you really are and how you lead will determine how pastoral staff and other ministries react to, and work with, your ministry. That bears repeating. As the head of an often controversial ministry, how people perceive YOU is how they perceive YOUR MINISTRY.

Executive Staff

Working with the senior pastor and any executive staff can be challenging and may lead you into serious conflict. Regardless of who approves of your team, and even with support from your church's governing board, if you do not work well with the senior pastor, your ministry will fail. Conversely, as long as you have the blessing and support of the senior pastor, your ministry will be able to succeed. In my tenure at Frontline, there have been a few times when my ministry has come under attack by other staff or board members, and often rightly so. It would have been relatively easy for my senior pastor to end the ministry. Thankfully he did not.

Because my pastor knew me personally, and because of how I worked with and reacted to the problems as they were presented, he was able to stand behind me in support and continues to do so. At those times in the past, I was assured that I had his support and blessing. Indeed, because he has seen my integrity and professionalism as we handle potentially ministry-damaging incidents, my senior pastor has supported our ministry even through any negative feelings or criticisms from staff, other ministries, or even the congregation.

As I mentioned in the first chapter, we went through a time where we were reviewing and possibly revamping our entire safety program. Through my fault and my lack of oversight of the team, I let the culture of the team become something unhealthy and unworthy of being called a church ministry. This was a pivotal point in the ministry. I would either lose all support of the senior pastor, or he would support the ministry and me personally in a leadership role. Fortunately, I was able to help him see the ministry for what it should be, for what it could be, and for what it would become.

What made the difference? As we were going through the review process, I had all the facts and figures present. I could justify everything I was recommending. Logically, I believed I had a "winning case." I was ready to go full speed ahead with the executive staff and the Church Board. In the end, none of that really mattered; everything hinged on my responses to the criticisms raised and the questions asked.

Throughout the whole process, I maintained as high a level of professionalism as I possibly could. I did not demand. I did not spread any of the issues to other areas of the church. I treated everyone as warmly and as well as possible -- even those I believed were wrong. Make no mistake, I'm not saying that I was a saint, or even that I was better than everyone else. I simply realized one over-arching truth: if I wanted to make sure that I landed on my feet, going in the direction that I felt called, and hitting the ground running, I realized that I had to hit my knees first.

I spent a long time in prayer and meditation. Afterwards, I was in such peace that I did not need to react badly. I did not need to spread the news. Instead, I simply needed to be who I was called to be, all the while treating everyone with the utmost care and courtesy. In the end, it was this response that allowed the senior pastor to see that I was worth supporting. As our discussions and reviews came to a close, I was thanked several times for my professionalism and warmth in handling the review. In truth, it was not me; it was God's grace that allowed me to offer grace to others.

If you have competence and training, but lack the character, leadership, and integrity of a servant leader, your pastor will have no choice but to withdraw his or her support. Without the servant leadership to guide you, all your training and competence make you a "security guard." Your church, and the church as a whole, does not need a security guard. They need servant leadership in a safety ministry. You must have the character, leadership and integrity to go with the competence.

On the flip side, if you have the character, leadership and integrity, but do not show the competence, your ministry will also end very quickly. While in some ministries, character, leadership and integrity may be all you need, in a church safety ministry, you and your team must have the competence to handle any safety-related crisis that appears.

If, however, you have the character, leadership and integrity of a servant leader, and add the competence and training for your safety ministry, you will find support from your pastor and staff. When you train and display competence in handling emergencies of all sizes, your executive staff will have the freedom and ability to publicly support and defend your ministry. As our team has handled incidents ranging from heart attacks to severe mental breakdowns on campus, our stock with the senior pastor and the executive staff has risen as well. In other words, our competence has proven that we are a valid ministry for the church community.

So what is the moral of this story? Your personal faith walk, leadership, integrity, and competence will determine your ability to work with the executive staff.

Other Ministries

Not only will your Safety Team Ministry have to work with the senior pastor and executive staff, you will also have to work with the children's ministry and the student's ministry in your church. To keep the children safe during services, most churches engage their safety team to assist the children's ministry leaders to help with check-in and check-out and to respond to the inevitable cuts, scrapes, or injuries that happen when kids run and play.

You personally need to be able to work hand-in-hand with the children's pastor and their volunteers. If they do not like you or trust you with "their" kids, your team will have a hard time making any impact and will be shut out of any planning. On the other hand, when they know that you and your team are there for all the right reasons, and can handle their emergencies, the ministry head will include you in their planning, their organization, and even their special events.

For a couple years at Frontline, we had a children's pastor that I did not get along with. Our personalities clashed in every meaningful way, and I'm not sure that this staff member saw the value of having a Safety Team Ministry. While I tried as much as possible to work with this particular pastor, I was met with nothing but resistance, and, at times, even encountered outright hostility.

When that pastor moved on and was replaced by a new children's pastor, I experienced a complete reversal. From my first meeting with the new children's pastor, I knew that she "got it." She understood who I was, and why I do what I do. Having come from a larger church with appropriate "security" measures in place, she was very receptive to making positive changes to keep "her kids" safe. We work together to give those kids a safe place to encounter God.

And what about student ministries? Your team will likely have a place even there. At Frontline, we are present when a certain threshold of kids are present, as well as during on campus all-nighters and special events. Like the children's pastor, I made sure to take the time to meet with the student ministries pastor to get to know him and to help him get to know me. There is nothing more frustrating than to be ignored and brushed aside when trying to help keep students safe at events. And there is not much more satisfying than being included in the planning of such events, knowing that they will be relying on your team to help them keep the students safe.

During worship services, you will also need to coordinate and work with the staff that is responsible for the services. Most modern churches have a worship pastor, music pastor, etc., who is also usually in charge of the technical side of things. This person may or may not have the responsibility of leading the greeters and ushers as well. As I've discussed previously, this is where I believe the church Safety Team Ministry really belongs or needs to fit. But, if not, you will have to work with these staff members and their teams as well. As with the other staff members and ministries, how well you are able to work with them is really dependent on how well you connect with them, and this will take time and effort.

Most churches place their safety team under the "Facilities" ministry. Whether your team is there or not, you will have to have a good working relationship with the facilities director and their teams. When you have a good relationship with them, there will be a healthy level of communication between you. This will help with notifications for emergencies, spills, and even security system and fire system planning and training. In your training, your people should be learning to also watch the facility. It will often be your team who discovers the small idiosyncrasies in the facility, such as the leaky roofs, the plugged toilets, and mysterious stains. Learn to help your facilities manager out when possible, fomenting good relations. After all, from major emergencies to mystery carpet stains, you are all on the same team.

One of the areas where you need to have a great relationship is with the administrative staff. Often overlooked, the church's office staff can clear large challenges for you or put huge roadblocks in your way. As a salesman for years, one of the keys that I learned early on is to get on the good side of any office staff, especially those who are the administrator for the head of the company. This applies directly to any office administrator at the church, and doubly so for the senior pastor's executive assistant.

This "gatekeeper" can smooth your way through the office and keep you informed of what your team needs to know, or they can poison your relationship to the senior pastor and church behind your back. While it probably would not happen overtly, if your notification of events or meetings was delayed or even forgotten, your team could suffer embarrassment or worse. If you want to work well with the staff, work well with the administrative staff.

Lessons Learned

In all of this discussion, there has been one recurring theme: You must be willing to sincerely engage and work with every ministry in the church. In other words, you must be willing to SERVE those leaders and ministries. You must be able to help the various staff and ministry leaders understand who you are, that your personal integrity is intact, and that you are competent for the position. Your entire Safety Team Ministry is dependent on how YOU interact and work with the other ministries.

The staff members must be able to see who you are, and where your passions lie. These staff members must be able to see that you are not trying to intrude on their turf. You cannot afford to get into a "peeing" contest over turf, and you cannot "mark your territory". You [bold]must[bold] approach every other ministry from a service standpoint: your team needs to help them serve their ministry. Through it all, your actions and activity must be sincere. Pastoral staff and ministry heads will be able to see through any insincerity, and this will affect your credibility.

I want to offer one important, throw-the-box-away type of advice here. If you cannot lead as a servant leader, or if you do not have the competence to train your team, you MUST rectify that as soon as possible, or you need to step down as the team leader. If you honestly do not have gifts in leadership, have some questions regarding your character, or even if you have a bad past in the church, I would recommend that you recruit someone to replace you as the head of the Safety Team Ministry. I cannot stress this enough: if you are not gifted to do the job and lead the ministry, find someone who is.

If, on the other hand, you do not have the competence and training necessary to get your team up to speed, that is a problem that you can solve. Humble yourself and bring in outside help to train your people. Your team will respect you more for getting them quality training than if you fumble through and fall flat in training them yourself. There is no shame in asking for expert help, and humility is a virtue.

The most difficult thing about leading the Safety Team Ministry is that all of this effort and work is usually a volunteer gig, without pay. This is the price to pay for a healthy, effective Safety Team Ministry.

Some questions to think about:

1. How well do you work with your senior pastor/executive staff?

2. Have you taken the time to meet with each of the ministry leads/staff? Have you gotten to know them and given them a chance to know you?

3. How can you improve on your relationship with the staff/ministry leads that you don't work well with?

4. What steps do you need to take right now to improve your connection with leaders in your church?

Notes:

Make a list of the ministries in your church:

(Now support them!)

Chapter 6

WHAT ABOUT THE BOARD?

Your Safety Team Ministry must work with the rest of the ministries in the church. From the senior pastor on down to the facilities and administrative staff, and everyone in between, your ministry must work well with the other ministries. In that list, there is often one area that can be a rather difficult team to deal with… the church board.

If you are just now setting up the Safety Team Ministry in your church, you will likely need to take it before your church board. If your team is already established, you still may have to submit reports to the board, or at least, respond to the board if any incidents arise.

Depending on your church management, there are typically two styles of board involvement. One style is where the senior pastor leads the church, and the Church Board is a group that provides a feedback and planning team for him, representing the congregation and other interests as the senior pastor leads the church. The other style of church leadership dictates that the Church Board has final approval and say over the ministries of the church, and the senior pastor represents them to the church, while taking the planning and approvals that they produce into his leadership. One way, the senior pastor leads, and the board assists with planning and represents the congregation. The other method sees the senior pastor taking orders and dictates from the board in how the church functions. Under either leadership style, your ministry will have to work with the board/governing body and will need to have their explicit approval and support.

Frontline Community Church operates with the senior pastor leading the congregation and the board acting in an advisory role, while representing the congregation. When I first brought the idea of commissioning a Safety Team to my senior pastor, he asked me to flesh out the details for him. When I met with him again, he liked what I was presenting and said that we would have to take it before the board. With the start of a new ministry that had the potential to interact with every other ministry, he felt that we should approach the board for approval. Because part of my recommendations were to have at least part of the safety team armed while on duty, he felt that having the board's explicit support would be warranted. Even when there have been a few board members over the years who were against having armed safety team members in the church, having the support and explicit backing of the board is very beneficial.

Like the support of the senior pastor, the support from the board must be kept through personal integrity and competence. The board must know that your heart is in the ministry. When there is an incident involving your team, you will need to have a positive track record and good rapport with the board.

You must take the time to meet with and cultivate your support with the board members. If you plan to have armed safety team members on duty, your board has to be willing to "take the heat." If your church board is of the style of having final authority over all the ministries in the church, then working with them is even more critical. With the other style, the support from your senior pastor can overcome some reluctance from the board, but your character, leadership, integrity, and competence must be well known. If your board has final say, and dictates their wishes to the senior pastor and staff, then it will not matter who is supporting you. If the board does not support you, your ministry is over before it has even begun.

How do you convince a reluctant board that your church should have a safety team? This requires a two-prong approach. First, you must come "armed" with facts and figures about church safety and security. NOTE: Come with enough information to be persuasive, but don't come across as being paranoid. There are reams of information available, so do your ministry a favor and do not overestimate the danger. At the same time, you will probably face reluctance from board members who are "willfully ignorant" and choose to bury their head in the sand. This is an absolute tightrope walk, and only you will be able to determine how much is too little or too much for the board to ingest. Your board must make rational decisions that they can stand behind because they will answer to the congregation.

You must also approach the board with a heart for ministry, and the experience to back it up. As we talked about earlier in this book, this must be a ministry from the start, and your board must be able to understand and relate to that vision. Your board members must be able to see your heart, recognize that you care for the church, and realize that your desire is to protect the church. If they understand your heart, they can accept the figures.

So what happens when you encounter resistance? When you meet with resistance, you must exercise patience, prayer, and a humble servant's heart. One of the most difficult lessons for me to understand was that I didn't have final say over what I thought the church needed. God has placed those folks on the board for a reason. If there is too much resistance, then they are missing something. I caution you not to assume that they are not seeing the facts and dangers that you see. Instead, their "no" may be a request for more information, or even a simple "not yet."

Lessons Learned

While training a safety team at another church, the head of the team approached me with candor and expressed frustration that he could not get the board to let him have armed personnel on his team. I counseled him to be patient. He was brand new to the position and relatively new to the church. I advised him to wait six months to a year before approaching the board again. This would give him time to build a reputation for competence, as well as let the board members get a chance to get to know him more. I believe that when he reintroduces the idea of some members being armed, he will be able to get the approval he desires.

Working with the board of any church can be frustrating. Those who are on the board are there because they care about the church. With rare, but glaring, exceptions, board members are there because they are serving their church in an area where they can help. They care about the welfare, ministry, and perception of the church. Give them the benefit of the doubt, and gently help them understand why your church is called to have a Safety Team Ministry.

Some questions to think about:

1. Does your board advise your senior pastor, or do they dictate to him/her?

2. Do you have the explicit support of your church board?

3. What can you do to improve your relationship with your board? With those board members who disagree with your team or policies?

Notes:

Chapter 7

DRESS FOR SUCCESS

What is your safety team wearing on Sunday? What do they wear for those special events that your church holds? How your team looks reflects on the team, the church, and, ultimately, can even affect how they act. For this chapter, I am going to assume that your safety team is visible, front and center, when people are on campus. If your ministry is completely behind-the-scenes and invisible, then most of this will not apply to them. If, however, your team is like mine, what your people wear can hurt or enhance your ministry to the church.

The Church Culture

When I first started planning for this ministry, I had to take the culture of the church into account for presenting the team to the congregation. Frontline Community Church is, and has always been, a very relaxed, young, post-modern church, especially when it comes to music and culture. Frontline serves a large, diverse group of people, and any "dress code" has been casual and simply "come-as-you-are." This means jeans and shorts are just as common as khakis, suits are rarely seen, and the pastors have even preached from the front in shorts and sandals. When I began setting up this ministry, no one wore anything with a church logo, and a plastic name tag was the most common means of identification.

I approached the team's look from a different direction. First, I redesigned and used a totally different style of name badge, visually cueing the team as different. Soon after that, we moved to burgundy polo shirts or button-down short-sleeve shirts with the Safety Team logo on the left chest. When asked about this shift, I pointed out that it set us apart and could be used in an emergency to let people know who they can contact. At the same time, special events started cropping up. I wanted a completely different, and much softer, look for events that were oriented towards those who didn't normally attend the church. And thus was born our "GIL" shirt.

Our Glow-In-the-Light (GIL) t-shirts are bright "safety green," that horrendously bright, light neon green that seems to shine even in the dark. Our GIL shirts simply say "Safety" on the back and on the left chest. They are called "Glow In the Light" because in bright sunlight they do actually appear to glow. We often get (very truthful) comments that people need sunglasses just to cut the glare. Why did I choose such a "different" color? Simple. I wanted the team to stand out in a crowd of people... anyone who needs help can find one of my team members. What started with joking comments has become a welcome sight at our events.

While our burgundy polo shirts have lost the "Safety Team" logo in favor of the church's logo, both shirts do the job they were designed for: they make us available to answer questions and help others. When I was questioned by one of the staff and a few of the board members about why I fought so hard to keep the shirts, I asked them to observe a couple Sundays, and then they would see. Sure enough, they observed what I already knew. We immediately became a go-to person for new people, or for someone who was looking for someone in particular.

Our visibility originally became evident to me while I was standing in a conversation with the senior pastor and the head greeter. The pastor had preached during the service that morning, and the head greeter was actually interviewed on stage by the pastor regarding volunteering. In other words, both men were up on stage with the spotlight on them for part of the service. As we were talking, I watched someone who had never been to the church before that day approach the conversation. During a lull, this person interrupted and asked me where I could find a particular room. The look on the senior pastor's face was priceless. After I directed the person to their destination, I pointed out that it was common for on-duty Safety Team personnel to field questions. Because I was in a polo shirt with the church logo on it and had a name tag, people naturally assumed I was with the church and could help them. I was also quick to point out that this happened with my entire team on a weekly basis.

After I made the challenge to some of the staff and board members to watch the interaction that we had with the congregation, several took me up on it, and I was quick to point out the instances that happened where we answered questions or directed newcomers in the church. Once they saw the results, they began to understand why I was adamant about the shirts, and the push to do away with the polo shirts and GIL shirts as identifiers was dropped. Instead, their usage was increased, and some budget was set aside to make sure all team members had polo shirts and did not have to purchase their own.

As a current policy, we have four different modes of dress -- and each one is designed specifically to maintain an appropriate level of presence at each event. First is our burgundy polo. Our "Burgundy" is worn for Sunday services, for most special church/missions events, and for covering most student ministries events. Our GIL t-shirts are worn primarily for three major all-hands events: Rockin' From The Roof, Easter on the Block (Easter), and Light the Night (Halloween). They are also worn at student over night events and for any coverage that we are providing for the township Farmer's Market that is in our parking lot during the summer. As a stark contrast, when there is a wedding or funeral service at Frontline, the safety team is present and the prescribed dress is dress clothes: shirt, tie and slacks for men, and blouse and skirt or slacks for women. By dressing up for these more formal occasions, we can show a level of respect to the participants. During this event-type, we only wear a small name badge to signify who we are. Finally, there are occasionally events and times that the team is in regular street clothes. This is specifically for events where we won't have a more formal presence but still want to be available.

Visible vs. Hidden

So why choose to be visible? There are two major advantages to being visible without being scary. First, by making your team visible, those who attend your campus will know who to contact in case they need help. It is often something as simple as being asked where the bathrooms are or finding a bandage for a child's cut finger. Occasionally you will be sought for a cardiac or respiratory distress event or other major first aid situation. When someone needs help, they need to be able to find your team. By being visible, you will be able to help more people.

The other reason for being in a visible shirt is to act as a deterrent for someone who is looking to cause trouble or act out. If a potential thief is looking for a crime of opportunity, a "soft target," if you will, then someone who is actively watching and is identifiable as working for the church will be a deterrent. This is true for the vast majority of "bad guys." According to all the studies, those "bad guys" who have no real specific plan to cause mayhem will move to other targets when someone is present and watching. Realizing that your church is a "harder target," they will often go elsewhere, and that is truly the best outcome. With the right attire and mannerisms, it is absolutely possible to be this deterrent to a potential criminal, and yet be the positive, friendly volunteer.

While I believe it is valuable if at least part of your Safety Team is visible and identifiable in some manner, there may be ample reason to remain in normal or street clothes. Do you want someone to sit up front to protect the pastor? Have them in everyday or Sunday attire. For some congregations, having a visible safety team may actually hinder the service and ministry. If so, leave your team invisible. Does the board need to ignore their presence? Then keep them in plainclothes. Your church culture will dictate whether they will have specific "uniform" shirts.

Lessons Learned

So what should your primary dress be? (And, by this point, I'm hoping you agree that it's not that ever-familiar light blue polyester.) Frankly, your attire depends on the culture of your church. If your church is a more casual, or a business casual environment, then a polo shirt would be a great solution. Professional looking, yet softer than a uniform, a simple polo with your church's logo on it will provide great visibility, with a friendly, professional appearance. What if your church's culture is that of shirt and tie, and usually jacket? At this point, step up into a long sleeve cotton button down shirt, and put your church's logo on it. A sharp looking dress shirt will certainly provide the crisp, clean, culture-appropriate attire that will place your team in good stead.

I know of a Safety Team at a "mega-church" that actually has all their Safety Team personnel dress in black. Their congregation has a history of problems, and they have a pastor that has enough notoriety to garner the attention of those who threaten to shut him up by using violence. In their culture, it makes sense to look more like "security" from the corporate world. For the majority of churches, having a polo shirt or dress shirt with the church logo will help convey a professional, friendly and available attitude. Whatever your choice, for your safety team, the old adage is absolutely true… dress for success!

A couple questions for you to ponder:

1. What is the culture of your church, especially as it comes to clothing and dress?
2. Does your team need to be visible, or are they relegated to behind-the-scenes? Some of both?
3. If they are to be visible, what would be appropriate?
4. Do you need policies for different types of events?

Notes:

Chapter 8

THE RIGHT TOOLS FOR THE JOB

I have discussed what the Safety Team Ministry should be, who you should hire, and even how they should appear to the congregation. What else does your team need to be successful in the ministry? There are several resources that your team should have access to, if they are going to be successful in their mission. Typically, those resources can be divided up between physical resources, the tangible equipment available for each and every mission, and personnel resources, the people and training available to you and your team members. If your Safety Team has access to both the physical resources, such as radios and first aid kits, and the personnel resources, such as leadership and community first responders, they will have the tools necessary to serve the ministry.

Communications

For success in your ministry, you will need to figure out

how to communicate with your team, and they with each other, before, during, and after your activities and events. The communications before your worship days or events will generally fall under two categories: scheduling and sign-in tracking. You will need to determine how often and which method you use to communicate your team's scheduling for events. Some methods that you might use include a wall calendar, printed lists, email/document files, scheduling software on the computer, or online scheduling services. Whichever method (or methods) you use, make sure that the information is clear and that you have a system for distributing the schedule to your entire team.

I cannot stress enough the importance of having the right person managing your scheduling and information. If your team grows beyond three or four people, and your team is active at many of the church events, you will want to have someone on your team that can do the scheduling and organization. If you are not organized enough to do the scheduling yourself, or if such organization is not one of your gifts, you will need to recruit someone for your team who can do the work. Early in my business career, I realized that this type of organization is not one of my strengths. When the team started growing, I knew that this was one of my weaker areas, and I found that I needed someone that I could rely on for the team scheduling. I have been blessed with someone who could really fit the bill. She is able to arrange all of the scheduling and coverage for Sundays, as well as special events.

When safety team members begin working at the church for their "shift," you should have a sign-in sheet or some other way of tracking who is on duty at any one time. This tracking is not for any punitive reasons -- it offers an objective accounting of who was there and when they were there. This provides a written account in the case of an incident where someone is called into question. Later I will discuss due diligence and mitigating risk, but, for now, understand that some form of tracking team members can be very worthwhile.

During your worship services and events, your team needs to be able to communicate with each other efficiently and effectively. In today's society where everyone has a cell phone, most churches would be tempted to have the Safety Team Ministry use cell phones as the primary way of communication during events. Unfortunately, this breaks down rapidly in a crises. With only one connection at a time, and a distinct lack of speed when connecting to others, cell phones have a distinct disadvantage over a radio-based service. Instead, cell phones should be relegated to calling outside responders in an emergency.

Rather than using cell phones, I believe that safety team ministries should have radio communications for the team. Smaller teams and churches can usually get by with an off-the-shelf collection of the "hobby" radios. The hobby radio solution is a relatively inexpensive solution, but the frequencies used are commercial Citizens Band (CB) channels, and anyone can listen or talk on them.

For churches that can afford it, and for larger teams and facilities, a commercial-grade radio system is really your best bet.

With commercial-grade radios, the frequencies are more secure and the radios and equipment are generally better able to withstand the use and abuse you will put them through. By shopping around for a local vendor who worked with other area churches, we were able to get competitive pricing and service. The commercial radios for our team cost around $450 each, with earpiece/microphones costing an additional $25 - $50 each. While this may be a large initial expense, the immediacy of instant radio communications in an emergency, and the durability of these radios make the Return on Investment (ROI) very worth it.

So who needs to carry a radio? Your safety team members, as well as at least one or two representatives from the children's ministry, should be your minimum listing of who carries radios during services. Your individual church needs, activities, and even building layout will further dictate who needs to be assigned a radio.

A word of caution: You will probably get some comments about "secret service," "security," or the like. This is VERY common and is usually handled one of three ways. When first approached and "teased" about the radios, most people will get defensive. Others may become embarrassed or ashamed of using them. I've even seen people simply stonewall and ignore the teasing. I recommend a totally different approach.

Train your people to smile, laugh, and otherwise enjoy the joke. Laugh with the person who makes the comments. Be quick to smile and joke about watching out for characters "just like them." Turn their teasing into gentle laughter WITH them. You and your team have been called to a sacred duty to protect your church and those who fellowship there. It is absolutely ok if some want to joke about it; in fact, it is very likely to happen. You and your team need to understand that those radios can literally help you save someone's life. Being able to take a little ribbing is worth much more than that.

After your services and events, your team will need a way to communicate any unusual or noteworthy events that happened during their shift. I recommend two different options, depending on the nature of the noteworthy event. A long time ago, I learned that an Incident Log is a great, informal way of putting on paper any unusual incidences, anything that did not at least require a full-scale incident report. This type of log allows the safety team members to read about incidents that happened and to be aware in case something similar happens again. The simplest form of this is a series of sheets with lines in a three-ring binder. The team members can fill out the log, and incoming members can sign off on it when they come in.

The second option, should the event require it, is a full incident report. An incident report accomplishes two very important tasks. First, it makes sure that you and your team fully understand the incident. This includes causes, remedies, and even suggested steps for improvement or avoidance. The second important reason to have an incident report is to provide documentation as an added insurance in case you need to provide it later to your pastor, insurance company, or lawyer. An incident report can be as simple --or as complex-- as you desire it to be, and I have included links to the one that I designed for Frontline in the resources section.

First Aid

One of the issues that your team will deal with the most is the necessity to provide first aid treatment to those on your campus. Everything from scraped knees in the children's area, to falls, sprains or broken bones with the youth, to potential heart attacks or strokes during service will all fall under your team's purview. Your team needs the best tools and training available to be able to serve the congregation. This is where the heart of the "safety" in the Safety Team comes into play, and this is where your team's ministry will have the most impact.

Depending on the physical size of your church, you may be able to get away with having only one first aid kit. I recommend that yours be better equipped than the $10 options at the local mega-store. If you look around online, you should be able to find a really good trauma-type kit for $50 - $100. This kit should be stored in a central location, one that is easily accessible. When mere seconds count, you do not want to have to hunt down a key to be able to reach the first aid kit. Make sure your kit is large enough to accommodate the supplies, and I would recommend one that comes in a soft-sided pack or bag, as these are typically easier to carry. If possible, get one that is brightly colored (red or orange) with the large white medical cross on the side. As with everything else you do, impressions are important, and a large, obvious first aid kit will give some credibility and even comfort to those you are serving.

If your facility is fairly large, I recommend buying several smaller first aid kits for the various areas around the building. These can be the basic $10 first aid kits, with a small collection of bandages, swabs, alcohol pads, and aspirin. In our building, our full trauma kit is supplemented with smaller first aid kits in the student area, children's area, and even in the sound booth in the worship center. This provides pretty good availability of basic bandages and swabs, while the larger trauma kit in the main lobby allows us to treat anything else.

One of the pieces of equipment that every church, no matter the size, should have is an Automated Electronic Defibrillator (AED). An AED device is a small, electronic shock kit that is simple enough to be used by even untrained people in the event of a heart attack. While "seasoned citizens" are the most likely candidate to need an AED, any person having a cardiac event will need one. While an AED may be an expensive piece of life-saving equipment, I believe there should be at least one at every church building.

Why is an AED so important? The Red Cross states that

every minute that someone whose heart has stopped is not hooked up to a defibrillator, they have about a 10 percent less chance of survival. It will take several minutes as a MINIMUM for a fire truck or ambulance to respond to your 911 call. When those precious seconds count, every minute will seem like an eternity.

At Frontline, the township fire department is on the opposite side of our parking lot. Even with the local fire station sitting across our lot, it would take those first responders a minimum of eight minutes to collect their gear, climb into the truck, drive to the church, find the incident, and finally hook up their own defibrillator. That is a long eight minutes, and the person would have about 80 percent less chance of even surviving the event. That is with the fire station sitting approximately 300 yards away, across a parking lot. How long would it take for your first responders to get to your church?

Safety Equipment

First aid kits and AEDs are only the first pieces of equipment that you should have on hand for your team. When someone from my team goes on duty, they have several pieces of equipment that they are supposed to carry. First, every team members is provided with an inexpensive belt pouch that contains at least one pair of latex-free medical gloves and a CPR mask. These pouches were less than $2 each (in bulk), and extras are always available. When you purchase these kits, also buy an extra box of gloves to replenish the kits -- your team will use these gloves more often than you think.

Next, you should have a number of small light-emitting diode (LED) flashlights for the team to carry. While the team members can carry their own light, we provide a number of them. The team carries these for two primary reasons: first, if there is a power outage, we can check the building more thoroughly, and get to places where emergency lighting isn't available; second, there are several places in our large building that are not lit normally, and we have the flashlights to enable us to traverse those areas, including storage and unused rooms.

The final piece of equipment that the team members carry is a small notebook. This is handy for writing down information while it is fresh. These notes can be used to give descriptions of lost items or children, help remember incident details, or for a myriad of other reasons. From my early days as a police officer, and throughout my time managing a security company, I always found that a small notebook for notes can help you recall most anything you need.

Not only do I recommend providing the basic glove/mask kits, flashlights and notebooks, you should also have a selection of traffic-style safety vests and flags or light wands. If your team ever works in your parking lots directing traffic or needs to be seen during evening events, a reflective vest can be the difference between keeping them safe and a tragic accident. Vests and light wands/flashlight cones are relatively inexpensive as an initial investment upfront. They also should last for a pretty long time, which will allow you to get the most return on the church's investment. If your team works outside at all, I really recommend that they have these tools.

Training

One of the most often overlooked "tool" that is vital for a safety team is training. While it can be costly, at times, the return on investment is exponentially higher. Some of the very first training that your team should receive is First Aid/CPR/AED training. By contacting local certified instructors, your team can gain valuable training, and, depending on your church's insurance, may even see some discounts to your policy by having trained personnel on staff. The least expensive type of this training is the basic "civilian" version, which certifies attendees with the basic proficiency. When budgets allow, I would recommend you get your team trained to the "Professional Responder" level of certification. This coursework will provide additional knowledge of response levels and better techniques that are used when working with more than one person.

Other vital training for your team should include basic ministry training which might include how to act and respond to others, what their demeanor and actions say about the ministry and how they should act, as well as what the goals and vision for the ministry are. Your training should also include basic tactical and strategic awareness, policies, procedures, and emergency procedures. Finally, your training should ultimately cover walking through scenarios of everything from a heart attack, to a child abduction, and even to a violent incident at the church. This scenario-based training will make more of an impact on them, and should be a part of every training session.

How often should you hold your training? My recommendation is to hold a formal, day-long training once a year. Then, depending on your team and needs, you should have smaller trainings semi-annually or even quarterly. Take the opportunity of the full-day training to make sure that your team is all on the same page, that attitudes are correct, and that the basics are refreshed. Your other, shorter meetings should be topical, timely, and worth the time of your volunteer team.

Much of your team's training can be held at the church with most of the training provided by you, or another expert on your team. As time and budget allow, search out valuable outside training that you or your team can attend. Even if you are the only one to attend the additional training, you can bring back what you learned to your team later and pass on the skills you acquired. There will be local, regional, and national groups that provide training as well as local law enforcement and even Department of Homeland Security training available in your area. All training is valuable, and most of it can be readily adapted to your church and your team without much trouble.

Local First Responders

Another overlooked tool that many churches fail to use is their connection to their local emergency responders including fire, medical, and law enforcement. You should make every effort to reach out to these folks and get to know them. Get to know the officers who patrol near your church. Talk to the local fire department, and make sure that they know you and your building. By getting to know these responders, they will also get to know you and your facility, and they will generally be able to respond better and in a timelier manner.

When I was first getting started at Frontline, I began contacting the local first responders. As I mentioned earlier, the closest fire station sits about 300 yards away from our building, across our parking lot, and this was obviously the first place to start. While our children's pastor at the time originally began working with the fire department to have them appear at our large events, I made sure that I worked to get to know the guys at that station really well. Over the years, they have found out that when we call for medical assistance, it is something that really needs a response, and they do their best to get there quickly. They understand that my team does have enough training to help them do their job better, which makes it a win/win for all involved.

At the same time, I started developing contacts in the local sheriff's department, as they are the law enforcement that will respond to any emergencies at the church. Through a team member who was also a training sergeant with the department, I also connected with the department's Tactical

Team (SWAT Team). After some talk with the lieutenant in charge of the Tactical Team, we invited the team to our building during the week to train. They do not often get the opportunity to train in large buildings other than abandoned schools, and they welcomed the change of scenery and practice. This not only enabled me to get to know the team but it also enabled them to spend some time in our building, giving them an advantage in case something terrible happens.

I firmly believe that by opening up and welcoming those first responders, you will see a tangible return of cooperation and an intangible return of ministry. Your actions with this ministry may be the door that God knocks open in the heart of someone who routinely sees the worst of people. Bottom line: build relationships with your local first responders.

Leadership

The last tool that your team needs is leadership. Biblical leadership is not about being the boss. Biblical leadership is servant leadership. You need to serve those who serve on your team. Servant leadership sets an example for others to follow. It is my policy that any criticism or corrections from the staff above me in the hierarchy are all filtered through me. The staff does not approach and correct my team directly. At the same time, I become the funnel for any questions, problems, or issues that the team has with other staff in the church.

Basically, it is my job to lead and train the team, and to

be the responsible, accountable leader and shield the team directly from any "stinky stuff" from the staff above. It is also my job to make sure that any needs or issues that the team has are addressed, either directly or by another staff member. With this simple philosophy, my team can serve where they are called to serve in God's church, and my job is to provide what they need to get the job done.

By taking responsibility for the team this way, I can shoulder any burdens that come down. I believe that servant leadership is there to take responsibility for any failures, but shares and reflects any successes back to the team. Servant leadership says that any of the team's failures are my fault. But, more importantly, servant leadership also says that any of the team's successes are the team's glory.

Lessons Learned

In this chapter I have included a laundry list of resources that your team will need, and WHY they need them. You need to equip your team to enable them to minister and to serve the church. Without the resources mentioned above, you will be sending your team to serve without fully enabling them to fulfill their mission and calling.

When I first started the Safety Team at Frontline, I did not have any of the tools above. It had been some time since I worked corporate security, and I had forgotten some of the tools that I needed. As we grew and matured, it took an incident where my team did not have something listed above to really drive the point home. In some ways, those experiences that generated the list of resources in this chapter also helped guide the initial direction for this book.

As I regularly take stock of what we have done and plan for future service, I continue to come back to the leadership component. I have seen teams succeed with a good leader at the helm. I have seen teams fail miserably with bad leadership. In rare instances, I have even seen teams succeed despite their bad leadership. But most of those teams do not shine unless that team leader is a servant-leader. Your team will need your leadership. If you cannot provide servant-leadership, please find someone who you can groom for the passion and leadership of the ministry.

Some questions to ponder about having the right tools:

1. Does your team have all the resources that they need to serve the church?
2. What tools are they missing? List them and then create a prioritized list to rectify the problem.
3. How can you better train your team?
4. Do you know your local responders?
5. Are you a servant leader? Do you help your team serve the church, or do you get in the way? Who gets the blame? Who gets the glory?

Notes:

Chapter 9

FIREARMS AND THE CHURCH

While talking about tools that your team might need, I would be remiss if I did not cover what is probably the one of the most contentious topics for church safety and security: firearms in church. If you have read any of my online articles, you will easily come to the conclusion that I support the arming of church safety personnel. I actually believe that churches should, if legal, allow anyone who legally can carry a firearm to carry them in the church. If this is not allowed, either legally or because the pastor/board doesn't allow it, I am in favor of arming select church safety personnel, and then equipping them with the best training. But why?

The Reason

Early on December 9, 2007, a gunman opened fire in a dormitory complex for Youth With A Mission (YWAM), a youth missionary training facility in Arvada, Colorado, killing two and wounding two. Later that morning, that same gunman opened fire at the New Life Church in Colorado Springs, killing two more and wounding three others before he was stopped. At the New Life Church, the only thing that stopped the killer was a volunteer. That volunteer had heard about the earlier murders and had volunteered for extra duty as a member of the church security team.

But what was different about that volunteer? She was licensed to carry a concealed pistol by the state of Colorado and had permission from the church leadership to carry in the church. She was able to employ her firearm and stop the killer before he could wound or kill anyone else.

In 2007, there were several church mass killings, including the New Life Church and YWAM murders. The difference between the other church attacks and the New Life Church killings is that there was a citizen who was able to respond even before the police arrived. It has been said that the brave citizen saved countless other lives that day by stopping the criminal.

The 2007 incidents are a microcosm of some very disturbing, and frightening statistics. Compiled by Carl Chinn, a speaker, author and church security consultant, statistics from January1999 through March 2013 show very disturbing trends:

There have been 649 deadly attacks on faith-based organizations since 1999, with 783 victims, claiming 339 innocent lives.

- 2007 had 41 attacks, 39 deaths
- 2008 had 64 attacks, 50 deaths
- 2009 had 108 attacks, 54 deaths
- 2010 had 102 attacks, 52 deaths
- 2011 had 107 attacks, 48 deaths
- 2012 had 135 attacks, 75 deaths

Almost every time that a killer has been stopped short of a larger massacre, it has been a volunteer at the church that has done so. Like the volunteer in Colorado, some volunteers have been armed and have been able to stop the would-be killer, while others have been forced to sacrifice their safety, and sometimes their lives, to stop evil. One unarmed usher was shot while stopping a killer after the murderer had killed the senior pastor In interviews later, this usher stated that there was no one who was armed to intervene, and this was because the church is located in Illinois, which, at the time, did not offer ANY type of concealed weapons permitting system.

Other than the occasional off-duty officer, law enforcement officers have largely not been involved in stopping these killers until the rage has run its course. Through no fault of their own, they simply cannot respond fast enough, and it is the speed and short duration of such incidents that cause the first responding officers to take more of a clean-up role than they would prefer. Most of these incidents are over within one or two minutes, and it takes longer for police officers to fully respond. Of the police officers and tactical (SWAT) officers that I have personally talked to, the vast majority, praise the fact that there are armed and trained personnel currently on campus to intervene until the police arrive.

In the state of Michigan, where my church is located, anyone who wishes to legally carry a concealed firearm in a church must have explicit permission from the presiding officials (typically the senior pastor or board). As I have talked about in earlier chapters, we are blessed with a senior pastor who "gets it." Part of my Safety Team is called the "Special Safety Team," and they are handpicked men and women who have the maturity, temperament, training, and qualifications to carry a concealed firearm on campus. Those team members on this special team are very carefully selected, and each one is trusted enough to have been personally recommended to the Senior Pastor and the Executive Pastor. Both pastors must approve of the new team member before anyone is authorized to carry a firearm while on duty for the safety team. With our Special Safety Team, we try to offer as much training as possible to maintain the ability and maturity to respond correctly.

I know of several large churches that do have armed personnel. Unfortunately, there are other churches that choose not to let any of their personnel carry a firearm on campus. In fact, I know of one large church that specifically forbids their safety team from carrying any firearms on campus. Due to their location, the church has had several incidents of violence that have started off campus and spilled over onto the church property. This same church has had several credible threats against their senior pastor, and these threats include death threats. In response, the facilities manager has assigned a couple of his safety team members to escort the pastor to and from his car every Saturday and Sunday. But, unfortunately, these brave men and women are unarmed. This cruelly turns them into mere cannon fodder. If there ever is an attack on the senior pastor, they will be forced to choose to throw their lives away, or to run away, leaving their pastor alone.

To Carry or not to Carry?

The issue of firearms in church is as divided among churches as it is among the nation. Typically, those who do not want guns in public places do not want guns in churches. On the flip side, however, those who have no objection to guns in general, typically have no objection to those who would carry while in church. Firearms are a polarizing subject in any polite company, and the church is no exception. In fact, I would say that the church is even more sharply divided. Whatever your personal opinion is, this is an issue that can cause severe divisions, even among church boards and staff.

So what is the "correct" choice? While I believe that a church safety team should have mature, trained members who do carry a firearm, each church must decide what policies would suit their unique culture. This is not a decision that should be made lightly. Instead, the leadership must prayerfully, carefully consider the options before them. While considering the matter, there are several questions that must be answered.

- Is it legal for non-law enforcement personnel to carry a concealed firearm in a church or on church property? If it is not legal for personnel to carry a concealed firearm, then this option should be discarded.

- Are there any law enforcement personnel who can, and do, carry a firearm in your church already? Law enforcement officers can be a great asset to any safety team if they are called and asked. If there are officers in your church, and if their personality makes them a good fit, enlist their help with the safety team, as well as for the training for any of the "special team." If you do not have any officers in your church, ask around and begin making contacts with your local law enforcement department.

- Are there any mature, trained, and motivated individuals that might be able to undertake such a role? They need to be heavily screened and have the best temperament for the various personalities and situations that the team will encounter. If you personally do not fit this description, you will need to find a mature, capable person who does fit the description to become the leader of this team, working with you directly to lead the team.

- If all of the prior questions are answered, then the final question must be asked: Does the executive pastoral staff and the church board approve of members being allowed to carry a firearm, and do they fully support the option? If the staff and board are not fully behind the idea, your team may run into unnecessary difficulties, or even encounter a loss of support. Whatever the choice, it must be with the full support of the staff and board.

If you have determined that you will have at least some members of the team armed, what should you look for in a person who will carry a firearm to protect the church? While it should not have to be said, they must be legally able to carry a firearm in church. Next, they must have a real maturity to them. Not only should they be "mature" as society defines it, they also should be spiritually mature. This person will represent you and the church, and possibly do so with a firearm. If they are not mature enough to make the right decisions, they may do more harm than good in the event of a violent attack.

In my opinion, the armed volunteer should also be someone who already carries a firearm everyday. Whether a law enforcement officer or simply a citizen who routinely legally carries a firearm all day, the person must be comfortable with carrying a firearm. When I am approached by a team member to be considered for our Special Safety

Team, my questioning inevitably leads to their carry habits. Do they carry a firearm every day? How do they carry it: concealed or open? Where do they carry it? What do they carry? How much do they practice? How do they practice? By answering all of these questions, I can understand their habits, capabilities, attitudes and desires. I can then determine if this person might be a fit. It should be noted that I have had to turn down some of the regular team members for the Special Safety Team simply because they never carried their firearm or did not practice much with it.

Any armed Safety Team members must have the desire and attitude to learn with training. If they are not willing to learn and do not take the job seriously, they will not be prepared if and when something happens. If they are not prepared, they can, and probably will, make the situation worse. While I believe that there should be armed members of any church safety team, I also advocate that these folks must be absolutely among your best people on the team. **Attitude, maturity, desire, and the heart of a servant must be present before someone represents Christ, your church, and you while armed at your house of worship.**

Lessons Learned

It is unfortunate that we have to consider the threat of violence against the church, but it is a reality in this current day and age in America. It is experience and research that indicates that the only way to stop a violent rampage in a traditionally "safe" place is to meet that force with like force

BEFORE and UNTIL the police are able to arrive.

My Safety Team has worked with the Kent County Tactical Team (SWAT) and the Lieutenants in charge of the team all heavily approved of having armed "civilians" on campus to engage and distract or stop threats if they happen until the police can show up. With the right personalities, training, and oversight, the Special Safety Team is a valuable part of the overall mission to keep the church safe for those who wish to encounter God.

For those who might question the scriptural validity of armed church members protecting the flock, I would refer you to Luke 22:35-39. In this passage of scripture, Jesus is talking with the disciples just before his last trip to the Mount of Olives and before his betrayal and arrest. He reminds them of their full reliance on God and how he provided for them. Then he tells them that bad things were coming and implies that they would be scattered. He then tells his disciples that they are to take their money bags, and, if they don't have a sword (ancient Israel's version of a handgun), they should sell their cloak and buy one. This passage and others seem to call, for the active protection of the church. In the resources section, I will also have a reprint of an article that I wrote exploring this concept more fully.

As you think about this chapter, here are a couple questions:

1. Is the senior staff and board willing to allow some of your key people to be armed?
2. What is the culture of your church regarding firearms?

Are the people from an anti-gun background, or are they used to seeing and owning firearms?

3. Are YOU willing and ABLE to lead a team with armed members?

4. Do you have anyone on your team who you would trust with such a weighty responsibility?

Notes:

What are the factors for arming your team?

Chapter 10

ONE LAST PRINCIPLE ... CYA

Forgive me for a bit of indulgence, but I need to add one last "principle" to our discussion. When I began working as a reserve police officer in Indiana, I was advised by my Captain to always maintain a file of copies of all of my incident reports, a "CYA" file, if you will. I began to develop a file called "CYA" in which I would store any incident reports that I filed. As I went into private security for a very large firm, I took that habit with me, and, as a manager, I maintained my "CYA" file as long as I was there. There were several times when that file saved me from discipline or even termination. I was glad my mentor recommended it then, and I strongly recommend similar measures for you and your team now.

This lesson is perhaps the hardest to learn, and is often the costliest to find out the hard way. When you and your team are helping keep your church and those who attend safe, one of the axiomatic rules that you must learn and understand is to cover your... backside. Known as "CYA" in more crude circles, you will need to develop policies for your ministry and train your team to serve the church while making sure that they are properly covered for mistakes and human frailties.

What do I mean by policies and procedures? One of the most important policies that you can implement is some form of an incident reporting system. I mentioned creating incident reporting forms in an earlier chapter, and I believe that they are very important. If there were ever an incident where law enforcement was called, having a written incident report would allow you to recall the details correctly and offer testimony for any lawyer, or judge, if a case goes that far. Also, today's litigious society encourages people to take any excuse to sue you, your team, or the church. By having written documentation of any such incident, your word will stand better than if you are trying to recall the events six months or even a year later.

I know from personal history that a properly documented and filled out incident report can help you with law enforcement and the courts. I have also experienced firsthand the importance of an incident report when it comes to the pastoral staff or church board. When your team's actions are questioned after an incident, the ability to provide a detailed, well-written account of the incident goes a long way in mitigating or resolving issues.

Policies and Procedures

Encourage your team to fill out such incident reports as completely as possible. You also need to remind and admonish your team to write each report as truthfully as possible - even if they made errors during the incident. Such documentation will only stand if it is true, complete, and accurate. If an incident does not warrant a full report, then this is where a log file is worthwhile. If the information is readily available, it will help you and your team.

When should you fill out an incident report instead of simply noting the incident in your log? Only you and your team can determine those guidelines. For Frontline, our rules are fairly simple: If it involves a minor or if emergency responders were called, then an incident report must be filled out. For all other incidents, when in doubt, fill out the form. This type of rule may generate a little bit of extra paperwork for you, but it will be worth it in the end.

What else can you do to cover your…tail? Craft smart policies that will, if followed, discourage frivolous attacks on you, your team, or the church. One important policy is to make sure that your team is completely "hands-off" any physical altercation. Unless you actually have sworn police officers on your team, your team members are NOT law enforcement. If they grab or touch someone, even a light touch to help escort them out, they could be charged with assault. Remember, your Safety Team members are NOT bouncers in a bar. Some latitude is given to bouncers as they break up fights and remove patrons from their bars. As a church Safety Team Ministry, you have no such latitude, nor do you have such calling.

If there is a fight on campus, your policy and training should mandate that they call the police and be good witnesses. Aside from our Special Safety Team, Frontline's policy is to avoid physical altercations unless a team member witnessed the start of the altercation, and they have to defend someone directly who is known to be the victim in the attack, and is weaker than the attacker. Even then, they are discouraged from engaging physically. My Special Safety Team will only ever engage if an attacker is using deadly force, and then they are trained to only go far enough to stop the attack in progress.

What other policies would be beneficial in helping protect your team? Only work with minors if the parent is present. In an emergency situation, make sure there is another adult available to stand by and provide witness. Just having another adult present, especially if they are a teacher or other safety personnel, will mitigate any potential claims. A corollary to this policy is to not have safety team personnel touch or apply medical services to those of the opposite gender, if possible. This is even more critical if the victim is a minor. According to most recognized media sources, the majority of "assaults" and abuse in churches today are sexual assaults or abuse. By maintaining proper decorum and having witnesses, your Safety Team should be safe from allegations of this nature.

Another vital policy would be to have a "No Comment" policy in place for press, and even with members of the congregation. In the course of working with the church members, you and your team will come across a great deal of personal information about those who attend. Your team must know that they cannot divulge any of that information, or even any of the inner workings of the team itself, to other members of the church. Make it a simple, carved in stone policy that all information and questions flow through you, the leader of the team. If your church ever does have a "press-worthy" event, such as a violent incident, you and your team MUST be trained to say, "No comment." Your team needs to understand that all of the information from the church must come from someone else on the staff, and they must never be the source of any information or speculation.

How is this Service?

I have spent this entire book talking about the Safety Team Ministry serving the church, and, to many, the above statements would seem to contradict that vision. I want you to understand why these policies and practices are just as much a part of serving the church as placing a bandage or saving a life.

If you or your team cannot effectively document any incidents, you, your team, or your church could be sued for large damages, or worse, possibly arrested and charged. It is part of your job, as a servant leader, to help protect and nurture your team. It is also part of serving the church to protect it from frivolous lawsuits.

The policies that you craft and train your team to follow are also part of the mission of serving your team by keeping them safe. All of these types of policies are meant to protect good men and women who are only trying to serve their church to the best of their ability. Working with minors or the opposite sex and gaining information are all part of the mission that is safety. Without such policies in place, you or your team might inadvertently cause more harm than good.

When the policies are in place, you must train your team to take those policies seriously. There is no benefit to having policies in place if they are ignored and dismissed. Hold yourself and your team to those policies - and if someone cannot or will not follow the policies in place, you may be forced to help them find another ministry to serve in.

Lessons Learned

It has been my experience that having such policies can help you serve your church. Every summer, our church hosts the local township's farmer's market every Tuesday and Thursday in our parking lot. As I was working on of those days, a car pulled up at the front entrance of the church, and a woman jumped out of the driver's side door as she screamed incoherently. While she was screaming and begging to see "the pastor" to "baptize" her, her daughter was pleading with her to stop.

As the woman became more incoherent, she began taking her clothes off, in public, in front of the church. With some help from a couple of the farmers, we were able to get her kids out of the car and away from the scene. By this time, I contacted the local emergency dispatcher, and they had officers and an ambulance on the way. I stayed with the woman, monitoring her and making sure that she did not go into the roadway, while the facilities manager for the church helped keep other people away from her and that entrance of the church. After an incredibly long 10 minutes, emergency responders arrived and were able to help her into the ambulance for care.

So what did our policies have to do with serving her and the church? Because we were able to get the information that we needed for the report, our pastor was able to follow up with this woman, making sure that she was getting the care that she needed. Because none of her specific information leaked outside the team or the senior pastor, she was able to start actually attending the church about three weeks after her breakdown. Two weeks later, she was baptized during one of our services. Because we kept her information private and served her like we serve everyone else, some of the staff who hadn't met her personally were unable to recognize her name when she was baptized. And two weeks ago, as I write this chapter, she approached me while I was serving on Sunday and personally thanked me for helping her.

This incident might have had a different ending if my team had not followed all of our procedures. In some churches, this lady might have been shunned, or simply felt too embarrassed to ever attend the church. Because we were discreet and served as a ministry for her, the senior pastor was able to follow up with her. When she came back to the church, she was comfortable enough to experience God. In the end, we were able to help her be open and available in a place where she could find the ultimate peace.

Take some time to ask yourself the following questions:

1. What are you doing right now to help protect yourself? Your safety team? Your church?

2. What is missing from your "CYA" policies?

3. What resources do you need to help keep your ministry safe? And how will you procure those resources?

Notes:

What resources do you need?

Chapter 11

SO WHERE DO YOU START?

If you have inherited your ministry from another leader, or have been working in the ministry for a long time, then this chapter may not hold much interest for you. Read it anyways. You may find something that you've been missing. If you are early in the process of starting your church safety ministry, this chapter is here to help you figure out where to start.

Step 1: Become a Servant Leader

As I have mentioned several times in this book, the person charged with developing and overseeing any Safety Team Ministry must be a servant leader. This first step is critical. The ministry can fail or succeed depending on who is the leader, the driving force behind the team. Reality in the church is that any new volunteer ministry must start with the right volunteer. This person must be an active advocate for the new ministry, must begin to organize and recruit for the ministry, and must be a servant leader in the position. It is hard work to begin a volunteer ministry in any sized church, and if the church is large, the roadblocks are larger.

As I said before, this ministry will be controversial, at best, and the leader must be someone that the pastoral staff and church board can trust and have confidence in. The staff and board must be able to back your ministry without reservation, and they must have confidence in you. You will need to have a servant's heart for the ministry, and they must be able to see that.

While not necessarily serving on the board or any committee, the servant leader must be recognized as a leader in the local church. The congregation must be able to trust you in that role, and they need to have confidence in your abilities and heart. A new member, relative "outsider," or someone with a history of failure in the church will have a difficult time in gaining the confidence and support of the staff and board, as well as the congregation.

This leader must also have very good people skills. You need to be able to talk to your friends, new attendees, and strangers with equal ease. You will need to manage your team members well, and you must genuinely care for people. This is a large part of the servant's heart. When you care genuinely, people will better respond to you. Whether it is correcting or training your team, or working with those on your church campus, genuine care will show through. Faking that care will lead to problems.

As a leader, you must also have good organizational

skills. Creating or reinventing any ministry requires a visionary leader, and those leaders are not usually the most gifted in organization. If you lack those skills, your first job will be to find someone for your team that you can trust to be organized. Your ministry will quickly run into trouble without good organization, and you owe it to those you serve to provide the best ministry experience possible.

As a servant leader, you must be able to recognize the skills and talents of your team members and encourage them to step up to meet their potential. This will often mean giving up some direct control over certain operations. If you have hired the right team members, and if you have helped them develop their skills and talents, they will be able to help you in areas that are not your strengths. You will actually serve them more by helping them take on those responsibilities. You cannot stand under the pressure to do ALL that is required; instead, help the people that God has provided fulfill the calling that they received. God has provided you with your team, trust him to use their talents for HIS ministry.

This leader should also be willing to connect with other leaders in the church, with other churches, and with local emergency responders. None of you are "competing" for the people you serve. Learn from others, and make those valuable connections.

Step 2: Plan for the Safety Team

Now that you are the right leader with the right

heart, your next step will be to do some strategic-level organization. The first part of this is to clearly define the ministry's purpose and philosophy. This is where you define the scope and actions of the ministry. In fact, this is where your ministry is either designed to serve the church or to simply provide security for the church. It is at this stage you will be setting the vision for the ministry.

It is also here that you, and the staff, will have to make some hard choices about the ministry. Probably the most difficult decisions is the subject of arming some of your safety team. This WILL cause concern, and will even possibly split the staff and board. As I recommended in the prior chapter, you must have integrity, character, history, and facts on your side of the argument, or this argument will be resolved before you have begun. Another hard decision that you must make here is the relative visibility of your team. Will they be in marked shirts, or will they be in plainclothes? If they will wear distinctive shirts, what will those look like? One of the last hard choices you will be making here is determining when your team has to be present in the building. Will they be there for every event? Will there be a certain threshold of people for them to be present? What types of events are they required for? All of these are hard questions that must be asked.

This vision/philosophy of the ministry should be clearly presented in a "Policies and Procedures Handbook" or similar manual. By codifying the vision in print, and then writing logical, well-planned policies and procedures, you will be able to communicate that vision and guide your team members as they serve. As an example, a link to a downloadable version of the Frontline Safety Team manual is listed in the resource section.

As you plan for your team, you will need to plan for the actual organization and hierarchy of your safety team. Who will lead when you are not available? Who will do the scheduling, and how will that be communicated? As you plan for the organization, you will need to figure out how to recruit new members of your team. Does your church recruit for volunteer positions in a certain way? How can you make your needs known? Then, as you recruit new members, your hiring process will have to be planned out, in detail, including desired skills, personality, and training. This requires a written job description.

Step 3: Budgeting for the Team

This step is vital, and it will drive you crazy because you have absolutely no control over the outcome. Several large initial purchases will all be competing for your budget attention, and your church will probably not have any funds budgeted for your ministry that first vital year. Unless there are any certifications required by the state, the budget needs can be broken down into two distinct categories: Training and Equipment.

For your training budget, the largest expense will likely be the First Aid/CPR/AED training for your team. Depending on the size of your team, this can be a rather large investment, but I would consider it mandatory. For equipment needs, the budget funding will be soaked up very quickly by first aid equipment (especially if that includes any Automated Electronic Defibrillators) and radios, with clothing coming in a distant third.

If at all possible, and if permitted by the pastor, contact a select number of church members to see if they will help fund this new ministry. This may take some coffee or dinner meetings, but a donor or two will certainly help ease the budget crunch. Because of certain dynamics at the time, the only way I could get any AEDs for Frontline was to approach a couple of donors directly. Thankfully, their giving allowed us to procure two AED devices for our 100,000+ square foot facility.

Step 4: Training

Once you begin your ministry, you will need to begin training your team members. I believe that the first two training sessions are absolutely vital. One of those first training sessions should be your team's First Aid/CPR/AED training. Your safety team must know how to treat injuries and medical emergencies if they are going to be able to serve the congregation.

The other vital training should be designed to introduce everyone to the vision and philosophy of the safety team. This should focus on policies and procedures, as well as strategic and tactical awareness and safety and security procedures, especially as they pertain to your building.

This training should also incorporate medical and violence emergency response procedures so that your team will know how to handle the situations. The last topic should be disaster response, including fire, weather, and seismologic emergencies. These emergencies have the most potential for wider-scale disaster and need to be covered with the other topics.

Other trainings should certainly follow, but I believe first aid and your policies and procedures should be right at the top of the list for any new safety team.

So where do you start? Start with a strong, servant leader. Define the vision of the safety team, and then plan to fulfill that mission. By then you will know what your budget needs are and can begin to gather those funds. Finally, as you begin, start with the basic training models to set the right tone for a successful safety team.

Take a few minutes to ponder the following questions:

1. Are you a servant leader?
2. Are you the right person to lead the team?
3. Is the vision and mission of the safety team clear?
4. Has the vision and mission been communicated in a straight-forward manner?
5. Do you intentionally remind your team about their mission?
6. How is your team organized?
7. Do you have clear, concise policies and procedures?
8. Have you been tracking and following your budget?

9. Are there members of the congregation that you can approach to help fund your safety team?
10. Are your people trained with what they need to know?
11. What can you do to help your team train better?

Notes:

Plan your team here:

FINAL THOUGHTS

When I began this journey, I was often questioned about the need for a safety team for our church. While Frontline is a fairly large church, our pastor is far from the most controversial in the area. Our church is made up of mostly suburban families and is in an area that does not usually see violence. There is no real history of domestic violence, and even our large children's ministry does not have a high injury ratio. Why in the world would a church such as Frontline need a Safety Team?

For most of my adult life, I have worked in one form of security or another, both physical and electronic. I was a member of my college's security force, including summer service there. I am a former reserve police officer from Indiana. I was a field manager for the largest private security firm in Indianapolis. I was a vault manager for an armored car company. I even worked fraud investigations for a major credit card company.

I have also been involved in the church for all of my life. Growing up as a pastor's kid, I attended school for youth ministry and served in various paid and volunteer youth leader positions in several churches, including my current church. In other words, I have a heart to serve the church.

Sheep, Wolves, and the Sheepdog

When I began heeding the calling to create and lead a safety ministry, I really had no words to express why I felt called to help protect the church, and those who sought her out. It was only a couple years ago that I read an excerpt from a book by Lt. Col. Dave Grossman titled, "On Sheep, Wolves, and Sheepdogs." I do not want to take your time and quote the entire passage here, but I would like to summarize some of the points that have had an impact on me.

As Col. Grossman points out, there are basically three types of people in this world. There are the peaceful sheep. They are not typically violent, unless they stampede en masse. They care about other sheep, and they enjoy their peaceful, blissful existence. To be a sheep is not, in this case, a derogatory statement. It means that the sheep is incapable of violence in most situations.

Then there are the wolves. These wolves like to prey on sheep. They use the fact that the sheep are defenseless and easily spooked to be able to eat their dinner. Wolves are violent by nature. Fortunately, only about one percent of the human population is wolves.

The human wolves enjoy preying on the sheep, and only have one natural enemy: the sheepdog. Sheepdogs are not shepherds - they do not lead the flock, they simply guard it from wolves. Sheepdogs accept violence only when it is necessary to stop the wolves. It is important to point out that sheep tend to not like the sheepdogs, because they have fangs like the wolf. Sheep usually ask sheepdogs to blend in with the flock because they don't like to be reminded that the wolves are on the prowl.

Digesting what I read, I realized that I am a sheepdog. I've been given the skills, talents, and backgrounds to help protect the flock. My belief is that sheepdogs are necessary for God's church. Sheep may not like having us around, but when the wolf approaches the fold, the sheep will all hide behind the sheepdog.

If you are called to lead, organize, or be part of a Safety Team Ministry at your house of worship, you are a sheepdog, too. Your safety team must be comprised of sheepdogs as well. As I discussed earlier, you and your team should all be *called* to this ministry and should have a heart for service.

Servant Heart. Servant Leader. Servant Ministry. Safe Church.

Not only must you and your team be called as sheepdogs, but your Safety Team Ministry must rise far above security and be a true ministry. It all begins with you. You must have a servant's heart. You must genuinely care for the people and the church that you serve. Genuine care will always shine through, and fake feelings will always be noticed. Learn to serve others and the church.

Your servant's heart will help you develop the leadership skills necessary to serve your team and church. The humanity in us all wants to shed all the responsibility for any mistakes that we may be culpable for, while accepts and enjoys any accolades that might arise. A servant leader will gladly take the criticism and responsibility for their mistakes, as well as for the mistakes of those who serve with them. At the same time, the servant leader is pleased to spread any accolades and glory to those on the team, especially those that might deserve it.

Servant leadership is infectious, and it will set the conditions for serving in ministry. By serving as an example to your team, they will begin to emulate the service and ministry. You will be structuring the ministry and setting ministry-oriented policies that enhance the ministry aspect of your team, while helping to quell any "security" tendencies from the corporate security world. Servant leadership directly leads to a Servant Ministry.

By truly serving as a ministry to your church and those in the congregation, I believe that a safe church is almost a given. As a ministry, your church will see care and service from your team, making it a generally safer place to encounter God.

Serve others. Stay safe.

Bryan Donihue

AFTERWORD

As my gracious editor was finishing working on this book, some changes happened with my team at Frontline. As I mentioned previously, I have been recommending to the pastoral staff that our safety team be incorporated into the welcome team personnel. Due to a recent staff change, our safety team operations were reviewed, and the great decision was made to shift the safety team from under facilities management over to the welcome team / FIT team.

This shift is occurring because I consider it a primary function to often evaluate the Safety Team Ministry at Frontline Community Church. I take the time to compare what we do and how we function to our mission. I consult with other members of the team and a select few members of the congregation about who we are as a safety team. I talk to the staff and get positive and negative feedback of our team. And then I compile the information and evaluate where the team is, and determine if there needs to be any direction changes.

As I've stated before, I believe that a Safety Team ministry will best serve as a part of the welcome/greeters team at the church. I have fought for this change in our own church, and am gratified to see it happening. I look forward to the future as we move forward to better serve those who come onto campus, and I will continue to evaluate our team to make sure we stay on mission.

This is a great reminder that, while the mission does not change, your team's policies, procedures and even placement may need to change to reflect changes in the church. It will never hurt to occasionally review your Safety Team Ministry to make sure that your team is ministry-based and mission-centered. It is the ministry that is the foundation, and that cannot be forgotten.

RESOURCES

In this resource section, I'm including several resources. Below is a list of books, websites and other recommended reading resources. Following this list are the two articles I referenced in the book. The first is one I published about Christians carrying firearms called, "The Dichotomy of the Armed Christian." The second was originally published in the book On Combat, by Lt. Col. Dave Grossman. In "On Sheep, Wolves, and Sheepdogs," Col. Grossman offers a look at the difference between the good guys and the bad guys, and what motivates the good guys to protect the innocent.

A list of resources and recommended reading:

Sheepdog Development Website

http://sheepdogdev.com

Frontline Safety Team Documents
http://www.sheepdogdev.com/request-church-safety-documents/

Contact info for training
Email - bryan@sheepdogdev.com
Web - http://sheepdogdev.com/who/contact

List of recommended reading:
Shooting Back by Charl Van Wyk
On Combat by Lt. Col. Dave Grossman
Stop Teaching Our Kids to Kill by Lt. Col. Dave Grossman
Crime Prevention for Houses of Worship by Chester L. Quarles and Paula L. Ratliff (American Society for Industrial Security)

Recommended websites:
http://www.carlchinn.com - Carl Chinn
http://www.copandcross.org - Cop & Cross
http://safeatchurch.org - Safe At Church
http://www.killology.com - Lt. Col. Dave Grossman
http://www.churchsecurityalliance.com - Church Security Alliance

Article

THE DICHOTOMY OF THE ARMED CHRISTIAN
by BRYAN DONIHUE

"Thou shalt not kill." (Exodus 20:13, KJV) This verse is quite possibly the most famous verse in the Bible about killing, and one of the most often used against Christians carrying a firearm. Another verse often quoted is from Matthew 26:52 - "Then said Jesus unto him, 'Put up again thy sword into his place: for all they that take the sword shall perish with the sword.'" (KJV) This verse is where we get the English saying, "Those who live by the sword, die by the sword". Yet another verse that gets thrown about is Romans 12:19 - "Dearly beloved, avenge not yourselves, but rather give place unto wrath: for it is written, 'Vengeance is mine; I will repay, saith the Lord.'" (KJV) The final passage is from Matthew 5:38-40 - "Ye have heard that it hath been said, An eye for an eye, and a tooth for a tooth: But I say unto you, That ye resist not evil: but whosoever shall smite thee on thy right cheek, turn to him the other also. And if any man will sue thee at the law, and take away thy coat, let him have thy cloak also." (KJV) As a follower of Christ who is supposed to "turn the other cheek", how can I justify carrying a firearm, possibly using a firearm against another human being, or even carrying a firearm in a church? Wouldn't that be against the Bible?

Short answer? I don't believe so. In this article I'm going to explain why these particular verses don't necessarily apply the way they are traditionally used, some passages I believe are also applicable to the discussion, and some thoughts on potentially spiritual issues surrounding Christians carrying firearms. No matter where your beliefs fall on the subject of armed Christians, by the end of this article I hope that you will understand why I believe that there is no dichotomy of being armed and being a Christian. To start off, let's talk about the four passages I quoted.

"Thou shalt not kill." Four simple words commanded by God Almighty to the Israelites as part of their original rules - the Ten Commandments. Except that those words were not originally in English. They were written in Hebrew, which has a very different meaning than the English words normally used. The "kill" part of this statement is the Hebrew word "ratsach". This word, while translated to "kill" in the King James Version (KJV), would more appropriately be translated as "murder". It is literally "unauthorized killing", from a root of "dash into pieces". This means that the English translation would more accurately, "You shall not murder." Murder is very different from self defense, or even war. If we were to take "thou shalt not kill" as a blanket statement, then all killing, including self defense, war and even legal execution of criminals, would be forbidden by God. Even a cursory reading of the rest of the Bible would indicate that war and legal execution are not only allowed, but even commanded at times by God. Instead, we must take an arguably better view based on the more accurate translation. Murder is forbidden, and this verse does not say anything about law-abiding Christians.

In Matthew 26, Jesus was in Gethsemane and a large group of armed men approached to arrest Him. As they approached, one of His disciples (Peter, according to other gospels) drew his sword and cut off the ear of one of the servants of the head priests. This is where Jesus tells the disciple to "Put up again thy sword in his place: for all they that take the sword shall perish with the sword." In other words, "Put your sword away, those who use the sword will die because of the sword." This is yet another problem with context. In this passage, Jesus has gone to Gethsemane to pray. He knew he was going to be sacrificed soon, brutally tortured and strung up on a cross. As He finished his prayers, He found his disciples asleep, and spent some time rebuking them. As Jesus finished this, His disciple, Judas, led a large armed crowd towards Him. They came to arrest Jesus, and one of his disciples decided to defend his Master. Peter's attack on the servant was an attempt to defend his Rabbi, not an assault without purpose. When he did, Jesus strongly rebuked Peter and healed the servant's ear. Jesus took the time to explain that Jesus knew He was going to die, and that He needed to go with the mob peacefully to fulfill His purpose.

So what about this statement? Actually, it is a pretty valid statement. If you take up arms to fight, you have a pretty good chance of dying violently. And yet, I do not believe this is a prohibition against carrying arms. Jesus himself did not forbid the use of the weapon, he said that he had to go meekly with the mob. Instead, I believe this passage is more of a caution. Carrying arms should never be taken lightly. It is a large responsibility, and it should be only done after careful consideration. Indeed, the rest of the Bible also has places where God's people are actually commanded to carry weapons, in and out of battle. So I don't believe that this particular verse actually prohibits the carrying of weapons. It is more of a precaution, and a warning to think carefully before doing so.

"Vengeance is mine... saith the Lord." This verse in Romans is a reference to another passage in Deuteronomy, and frankly, is one of the least powerful in the argument against Christians carrying weapons. There is a common willful ignorance among those who do not like firearms and a belief that those civilians who carry guns are either "playing Rambo" or "itching for revenge". Nothing could be further from the truth. Most lawful firearm carriers honestly never want to use their gun to kill a human. Most of us enjoy shooting at the range and training with our firearm, but we never want to be forced to use it against another human being.

This verse, and the corresponding verse in Deuteronomy are not about lawful acts. They are not about war, law enforcement, or even self defense. They are about revenge. In these passages, and in others throughout the Bible, Christians are told to "forgive" those who harm them. We are admonished to be nice to those who hurt us. It is very clear that God is the sole arbiter of revenge. He gets to choose how vengeance is distributed, and we have no part of that domain. I need to make something very clear here: If a Christian uses a weapon to exact revenge on anyone, for any purpose, that vengeance is not in God's will. Vengeance is God's domain only, not ours. On the other hand, defending yourself from a current attack, defending your family, enforcing the laws are NOT motivated by revenge. War should never be motivated by revenge, that would not be a "just war". Using a firearm in the defense of the innocent is not vengeance, it is simply defense.

We finally come to the passage that is often the most misunderstood and misused passage against Christians defending themselves or their loved ones. The concept of "turn the other cheek" comes from Matthew 5, commonly called "The Beatitudes". In this passage, Jesus is addressing a large crowd, and talking about the Jewish law, and explaining that it is the spirit of the laws that are important, not just the letters of the law. Jesus talks about the laws saying that if someone is harmed, the criminal is to get harmed in the same way. Jesus says that we are not to resist the evil, and if someone strikes us on the right cheek, then we are to allow them to strike the other cheek. Also, if someone sues us for our shirt, we are to give them our coat as well. And finally, someone forces us to walk a mile for them, we should instead go two.

As with previous passages, context is the key to understanding what this passage means. As Jesus begins talking, He admonishes us not to resist "poneros" which is properly translated an "evildoer", or even "the evil one" (the devil). He then modifies this statement with the three following conditions. First, if we are struck on the "right cheek", we are to calmly offer the left. This is not about defense. The original greek term for the hitting or slapping is "rhapizo", which means to slap (with an open hand). If you are "rhapizo" (slapped) on the right cheek, the person who slapped you did so with their LEFT hand. The left hand in that culture was the "unclean" hand, as it was the one used to wipe up after using the bathroom. In other words, this is not a violent attack, it is considered an insult. This verse tells us to ignore open insults, and not to react. Second, we are told that if we are sued for our shirt, we should simply give up our coat as well. This admonishment tells us to not worry about minor insults or lawsuits from non-believers. Finally, what about this "walk a mile" for someone? When Jesus lived, the Israelites were under Roman rule. There was a law on the books that said a Roman soldier could force a Jewish citizen work or carry a load for up to a mile at any time. Jesus tells us that Christians are supposed to respond to this insult by carrying the load for two miles without being asked.

Everyone of these conditional statements is reflected by the "do not resist the evildoer" statement. With a little digging and background, it is apparent that Jesus was talking about handling smaller insults graciously. It is be illogical, unethical, and illegal to respond to a mere insult with a weapon or a fight. It is wrong to respond to a simple, legal command with grumbling and bad attitude. This passage in Matthew is teaching Christians how to respond to minor insults. We are supposed to respond with grace and mercy. We are told to respond with character. This is even more important for those of us who choose to be legally armed.

As a legally armed citizen, I have to be even more careful about how I respond to insults, threats, and everyday annoyances. The simple act of wearing a firearm can turn any aggressive action or fight into an assault, and will quickly turn an over-reaction into jail time. When a firearm is introduced, road rage can turn into assault with a deadly weapon. Most armed citizens recognize this. When you add this passage from Matthew, as an armed Christian, the strong recommendation from a legal perspective turns into a command from God. We curb our temper. We ignore insults. We act graciously when we need to. As a responsibly armed Christian, I have to be extra careful and gracious when I'm insulted or mistreated. Other responsibly armed Christians have told me that they have found the same thing. In fact, I would wager that a large percentage of legally armed Christians are actually more gracious when dealing with insults than others simply because they know that they have more to lose than the average unarmed Christian. However, nothing in this passage deals with responding to criminals or defending yourself or your loved ones.

So what Biblical passages do Christians turn to when they want to consider being armed? Are there any that might suggest it is ok to defend the church? I would submit a couple of passages for your consideration: Nehemiah 4, Exodus 22:1-2, and Luke 22:35-38. And as above, context and the original language are the keys to deciphering these passages.

In Nehemiah 4, the Israelites are rebuilding the city of Jerusalem, and specifically the wall around the city. As they are building, they are being harassed by the surrounding cities and states. With negotiations failing, the prophet Nehemiah orders the workers to carry their weapons with them. When they heard that they were going to be attacked, Nehemiah placed all the armed families on the wall (v. 13). After their enemies slunk away without attacking, workers were divided up and armed. At any one time, half of the workers were armed, and half were working (v. 16). The passage then goes on to describe that the builders worked with one hand on their bricks and one hand on their swords (v. 17-18). Why is this important? It shows that armed defense, according to God's will, can be a good thing. In fact, when the enemies found out that the families (men and women) were armed, they never even attacked. It seems to me that there may be a modern day parallel to the church there.

Exodus 22 is a passage concerning the property rights and the legal response to criminals. This passage gets a little complicated to unravel, but the context and principles are extremely relevant and appropriate today. Verses 2-3 state, "If a thief be found breaking up, and be smitten that he die, there shall no blood be shed for him. If the sun be risen upon him, there shall be blood shed for him; for he should make full restitution; if he have nothing, then he shall be sold for his theft." (KJV) So what does this mean? The NLT version speaks it a bit more plainly: "If a thief is caught in the act of breaking into a house and is struck and killed in the process, the person who killed the thief is not guilty of murder. But if it happens in daylight, the one who killed the thief is guilty of murder. A thief who is caught must pay in full for everything he stole. If he cannot pay, he must be sold as a slave to pay for his theft."

This text speaks to Jewish laws regarding bloodguilt. In Jewish society, if a person was murdered, or wrongfully killed, there was a bloodguilt, or blood debt placed on the killer, and the punishment was very often death. However, if there was no bloodguilt associated with taking the life, the person was innocent, and could not be forced to pay restitution. This passage talks about thieves breaking into the house (literally breaking through the wall of the houses). It was law that if you caught a thief breaking into your house at night, when it was dark, it was ok to kill them. If the homeowner did kill them, and they were merely a thief, the homeowner would not face bloodguilt because it was too dark to tell the difference between a thief and a murderer. However, if it was daylight, and the thief was discovered taking something, they were not to be killed. Instead, they were to be forced to pay restitution, and sold into slavery if they could not pay the restitution. Here, if the homeowner knew that it was a thief, and not a murderer, there was no justification to kill over the taking of "stuff".

I want to make sure that you understand the nuances of this passage. The biblical concept is that if a person is attacking you or your family, it is okay to defend your family, even if it means killing the aggressor. However, if a person is merely taking your stuff, it is not okay to kill them. Capture them? Yes. Make them pay restitution? Absolutely. Kill them for taking stuff? Not according to God's laws.

I believe that this passage applies even today. If someone is merely taking your stuff, and not really threatening you, it really is not ok, according to this passage, to respond with deadly force. However, if a person is attacking you, it is ok according to Biblical law, to defend your self and your family. What if you are unsure of the criminal's motives? This begins to walk a fine line, and you will need to let your conscious and the Holy Spirit guide your response.

Finally, we look at another telling of Jesus at Gethsemane. In Luke 22:35-38 we read: "And he [Jesus] said unto them, 'When I sent you without purse, and scrip, and shoes, lacked ye any thing?' And they said, 'Nothing.' Then said he unto them, 'But now, he that hath a purse, let him take it, and likewise his scrip: and he that hath no sword, let him sell his garment, and buy one. For I say unto you, that this that is written must yet be accomplished in me, And he was reckoned among the transgressors: for the things concerning me have an end.' And they said, 'Lord, behold, here are two swords. And he said unto them, It is enough.'" (KJV)

This discussion takes place just before Judas leads an angry mob to arrest Jesus. Here Jesus reminds the disciples that He had already sent them out with nothing so that they learned to rely on God for everything (v. 35). He then says to them, "Now is the time to gather your stuff. You will be scattered and traveling. Make sure you have money. And if you do not have a sword, sell your clothes to buy one." (v. 36) A moment later, they produce two swords, and Jesus tells them that they have enough protection (v. 38).

I believe that there are a couple take-aways from this passage. In that time, the short sword, or common sword, was the basic defensive weapon of the day, much like our modern handgun. The fact that Jesus is telling his disciples that they need to be able to defend themselves is interesting, and spoke volumes about what was coming for His followers. Keep in mind, the timing of this conversation. In just a few moments, Judas is going to be leading an angry mob up the hill, and Peter is going to lop the ear off of one of the priests servants, earning a stunning rebuke in the process. Jesus just told his disciples to arm themselves, yet they are not supposed to use it to defend Jesus? No. Jesus knows that he has to be crucified to become the blood sacrifice for the whole world's sin. He is going willingly. This means that the swords were there for the disciples defense while they are out on the road.

Another interesting fact is that a mere two swords satisfy Jesus' command to buy swords. Only two of the eleven disciples will be armed, but Jesus calls that "enough". What I find interesting in this passage is that only 18% of the population needed to be armed to have an adequate defense. Two out of eleven was "enough". Modern studies have shown that not everyone has to be armed to see a lessening of violent crime. However, when people are armed, the overall rate of violent crime decreases. In fact, only a relatively small portion of society needs to actually be armed for this trend to appear. I believe the church as a whole does not need to have everyone armed, just a select few who are able, and willing, to defend the church against danger.

Finally, we might draw a conclusion that there is a time to fight and defend yourself, and there is a time to go gently and meekly to your grave. All of this depends on God's will. Jesus knew that he had to fulfill the sacrifice and die on the cross. He went mildly with the mob, not offering offense, screaming curses, or even pleading for His life. He knew that his job was to go quietly. On the other hand, he sent His disciples out into the world armed for defense. This passage hints that it is okay to use a weapon sometimes, as long as you are following God's will.

I believe the difference between carrying a firearm as a Christian, and not carrying one is the person's definition of "Righteous Violence". Is it ever ok to be violent? Christ himself got violent when he saw the mockery that the moneychangers had made of the temple courtyard. The Greek words used describe a very violent fit of rage, throwing tables and using whips on the vendors. I believe that there may be times when violence is righteous, and at even necessary. One of those times is in defense of the church itself.

I believe that the church has the Biblical authority, and possibly even a mandate to respond and defend themselves. I believe that we are called to defend the flock from predators. Sometimes this is a simple conversation. Sometimes it means putting the right safeguards in place. And sometimes it means responding to violent attacks with a tempered violent defense. As long as the defense is measured, appropriate, and under God's Will, the church has the authority to defend the flock.

This begs the question - is it ever ok to kill someone while defending yourself, your family or your church? I believe I've shown the answer to be a qualified, "Yes". As long as the defense is not revenge, and as long as the people of the church are threatened, I believe that it is ok to respond with deadly force. On the other hand, if the criminal is simply taking "stuff", a violent response is neither called for, nor acceptable to defend the church.

By extension, I believe the same applies to families

and individuals as well. Parents, fathers and mothers, are charged throughout the Bible to protect the family and raise the family correctly. That is our purpose. There are enough places in the Bible to explore the fact that sometimes the raising of children may also be in training them how to make war.

I would like to bring up one final question for those who believe that Christians should not carry a firearm, and especially not while in church. If it is not Biblical for a Christian to carry a firearm, then how do you look at those who serve in law enforcement or the military? A logical thought process would take any restrictions on Christians being armed to the next step that there should not be any Christian police officers or military personnel. After all, the scriptures that you might quote do not say "unless your job requires it." If someone does not believe that Christians should be armed, then they cannot logically accept any Christian law enforcement or military personnel.

On the other hand, if it is ok for Christian law enforcement or military personnel to carry a firearm, and even to kill "enemies", then why must a "citizen" Christian be disarmed. And remember, job description does not make a sin into a virtue. The argument that it is part of their "job" is not a valid SCRIPTURAL argument. I have met many thoughtful, caring, and I believe misguided, Christians who are terrified of firearms in church or being owned and carried by other Christians, yet have no problem with an armed Christian police officer or member of the military. While misguided, these people tend to have the best of intentions, but the logical fallacies compound with the scriptural fallacies and create an uneducated and unprotected church.

What about me? I have chosen to carry a firearm everywhere I legally can. While I sometimes carry the handgun openly in a holster on my hip, I most often carry my firearm concealed from the public. I long ago made a decision that it is my Christian duty to defend myself, my family, and even the church from the predators that prowl in the world. This means that I train to be able and capable to defend my family's life as necessary. The vast majority of people who meet me on the street, or know me casually, will never know that I am legally carrying a firearm. I carry it to defend myself, my family, and yes, even my church.

The definition of Dichotomy is: "A division into two parts or classifications, especially when they are sharply distinguished or opposed." Most people would consider an armed Christian to be a dichotomy, at least on the surface. The church has a history of emphasizing the passivity and meekness of Christ, and carrying a firearm is not associated with meekness and passivity. As we look at the scripture references in this article, we see that being a Christian and being armed and able to defend your family and church are NOT mutually exclusive. In fact, I believe the Bible shows that being an armed Christian can actually be a calling as well.

NOTE: This article can be found in its original format at
http://sheepdogdev.com/soapbox/108-dichotomy

Article

ON SHEEP, WOLVES, AND SHEEPDOGS
by LT. COL. DAVE GROSSMAN

*The following excerpt is taken from the book **On Combat** by Lt. Col. Dave Grossman with gracious permission from the author.*

One Vietnam veteran, an old retired colonel, once said this to me: "Most of the people in our society are sheep. They are kind, gentle, productive creatures who can only hurt one another by accident." This is true. Remember, the murder rate is six per 100,000 per year, and the aggravated assault rate is four per 1,000 per year. What this means is that the vast majority of Americans are not inclined to hurt one another.

Some estimates say that two million Americans are victims of violent crimes every year, a tragic, staggering number, perhaps an all-time record rate of violent crime. But there are almost 300 million Americans, which means that the odds of being a victim of violent crime is considerably less than one in a hundred on any given year.

Furthermore, since many violent crimes are committed by repeat offenders, the actual number of violent citizens is considerably less than two million.

Thus there is a paradox, and we must grasp both ends of the situation: We may well be in the most violent times in history, but violence is still remarkably rare. This is because most citizens are kind, decent people who are not capable of hurting each other, except by accident or under extreme provocation. They are sheep.

I mean nothing negative by calling them sheep. To me it is like the pretty, blue robin's egg. Inside it is soft and gooey but someday it will grow into something wonderful. But the egg cannot survive without its hard blue shell. Police officers, soldiers and other warriors are like that shell, and someday the civilization they protect will grow into something wonderful. For now, though, they need warriors to protect them from the predators.

"Then there are the wolves," the old war veteran said, "and the wolves feed on the sheep without mercy." Do you believe there are wolves out there who will feed on the flock without mercy? You better believe it. There are evil men in this world and they are capable of evil deeds. The moment you forget that or pretend it is not so, you become a sheep. There is no safety in denial.

"Then there are sheepdogs," he went on, "and I'm a sheepdog. I live to protect the flock and confront the wolf." Or, as a sign in one California law enforcement agency put it, "We intimidate those who intimidate others."

If you have no capacity for violence then you are a healthy productive citizen: a sheep. If you have a capacity for violence and no empathy for your fellow citizens, then you have defined an aggressive sociopath--a wolf. But what if you have a capacity for violence, and a deep love for your fellow citizens? Then you are a sheepdog, a warrior, someone who is walking the hero's path. Someone who can walk into the heart of darkness, into the universal human phobia, and walk out unscathed.

The gift of aggression

Everyone has been given a gift in life. Some people have a gift for science and some have a flair for art. And warriors have been given the gift of aggression. They would no more misuse this gift than a doctor would misuse his healing arts, but they yearn for the opportunity to use their gift to help others. These people, the ones who have been blessed with the gift of aggression and a love for others, are our sheepdogs. These are our warriors.

One career police officer wrote to me about this after attending one of my Bulletproof Mind training sessions:

"I want to say thank you for finally shedding some light on why it is that I can do what I do. I always knew why I did it. I love my [citizens], even the bad ones, and had a talent that I could return to my community. I just couldn't put my finger on why I could wade through the chaos, the gore, the sadness, if given a chance try to make it all better, and walk right out the other side."

Let me expand on this old soldier's excellent model of the sheep, wolves, and sheepdogs. We know that the sheep live in denial; that is what makes them sheep. They do not want to believe that there is evil in the world. They can accept the fact that fires can happen, which is why they want fire extinguishers, fire sprinklers, fire alarms and fire exits throughout their kids' schools. But many of them are outraged at the idea of putting an armed police officer in their kid's school. Our children are dozens of times more likely to be killed, and thousands of times more likely to be seriously injured, by school violence than by school fires, but the sheep's only response to the possibility of violence is denial. The idea of someone coming to kill or harm their children is just too hard, so they choose the path of denial.

The sheep generally do not like the sheepdog. He looks a lot like the wolf. He has fangs and the capacity for violence. The difference, though, is that the sheepdog must not, cannot and will not ever harm the sheep. Any sheepdog who intentionally harms the lowliest little lamb will be punished and removed. The world cannot work any other way, at least not in a representative democracy or a republic such as ours.

Still, the sheepdog disturbs the sheep. He is a constant reminder that there are wolves in the land. They would prefer that he didn't tell them where to go, or give them traffic tickets, or stand at the ready in our airports in camouflage fatigues holding an M-16. The sheep would much rather have the sheepdog cash in his fangs, spray paint himself white, and go, "Baa."

Until the wolf shows up. Then the entire flock tries desperately to hide behind one lonely sheepdog. As Kipling said in his poem about "Tommy" the British soldier:

While it's Tommy this, an' Tommy that, an' "Tommy, fall be'ind,"
But it's "Please to walk in front, sir," when there's trouble in the wind,
There's trouble in the wind, my boys, there's trouble in the wind,
O it's "Please to walk in front, sir," when there's trouble in the wind.

- "Tommy" by Rudyard Kipling

The students, the victims, at Columbine High School were big, tough high school students, and under ordinary circumstances they would not have had the time of day for a police officer. They were not bad kids; they just had nothing to say to a cop. When the school was under attack, however, and SWAT teams were clearing the rooms and hallways, the officers had to physically peel those clinging, sobbing kids off of them. This is how the little lambs feel about their sheepdog when the wolf is at the door. Look at what happened after September 11, 2001, when the wolf pounded hard on the door. Remember how America, more than ever before, felt differently about their law enforcement officers and military personnel? Remember how many times you heard the word hero?

Understand that there is nothing morally superior about being a sheepdog; it is just what you choose to be. Also understand that a sheepdog is a funny critter: He is always sniffing around out on the perimeter, checking the breeze, barking at things that go bump in the night, and yearning for a righteous battle. That is, the young sheepdogs yearn for a righteous battle. The old sheepdogs are a little older and wiser, but they move to the sound of the guns when needed right along with the young ones.

Here is how the sheep and the sheepdog think differently. The sheep pretend the wolf will never come, but the sheepdog lives for that day. After the attacks on September 11, 2001, most of the sheep, that is, most citizens in America said, "Thank God I wasn't on one of those planes." The sheepdogs, the warriors, said, "Dear God, I wish I could have been on one of those planes. Maybe I could have made a difference." When you are truly transformed into a warrior and have truly invested yourself into warriorhood, you want to be there. You want to be able to make a difference.

While there is nothing morally superior about the sheepdog, the warrior, he does have one real advantage. Only one. He is able to survive and thrive in an environment that destroys 98 percent of the population.

There was research conducted a few years ago with individuals convicted of violent crimes. These cons were in prison for serious, predatory acts of violence: assaults, murders and killing law enforcement officers. The vast majority said that they specifically targeted victims by body language: slumped walk, passive behavior and lack of awareness. They chose their victims like big cats do in Africa, when they select one out of the herd that is least able to protect itself.

However, when there were cues given by potential victims that indicated they would not go easily, the cons said that they would walk away. If the cons sensed that the target was a "counter-predator," that is, a sheepdog, they would leave him alone unless there was no other choice but to engage.

One police officer told me that he rode a commuter train to work each day. One day, as was his usual, he was standing in the crowded car, dressed in blue jeans, T-shirt and jacket, holding onto a pole and reading a paperback. At one of the stops, two street toughs boarded, shouting and cursing and doing every obnoxious thing possible to intimidate the other riders. The officer continued to read his book, though he kept a watchful eye on the two punks as they strolled along the aisle making comments to female passengers, and banging shoulders with men as they passed.

As they approached the officer, he lowered his novel and made eye contact with them. "You got a problem, man?" one of the IQ-challenged punks asked. "You think you're tough, or somethin'?" the other asked, obviously offended that this one was not shirking away from them.

"As a matter of fact, I am tough," the officer said, calmly and with a steady gaze.

The two looked at him for a long moment, and then without saying a word, turned and moved back down the aisle to continue their taunting of the other passengers, the sheep.

Some people may be destined to be sheep and others might be genetically primed to be wolves or sheepdogs. But I believe that most people can choose which one they want to be, and I'm proud to say that more and more Americans are choosing to become sheepdogs.

Seven months after the attack on September 11, 2001, Todd Beamer was honored in his hometown of Cranbury, New Jersey. Todd, as you recall, was the man on Flight 93 over Pennsylvania who called on his cell phone to alert an operator from United Airlines about the hijacking. When he learned of the other three passenger planes that had been used as weapons, Todd dropped his phone and uttered the words, "Let's roll," which authorities believe was a signal to the other passengers to confront the terrorist hijackers. In one hour, a transformation occurred among the passengers--athletes, business people and parents--from sheep to sheepdogs and together they fought the wolves, ultimately saving an unknown number of lives on the ground.

Here is the point I like to emphasize, especially to the thousands of police officers and soldiers I speak to each year. In nature the sheep, real sheep, are born as sheep. Sheepdogs are born that way, and so are wolves. They didn't have a choice. But you are not a critter. As a human being, you can be whatever you want to be. It is a conscious, moral decision.

If you want to be a sheep, then you can be a sheep and that is okay, but you must understand the price you pay. When the wolf comes, you and your loved ones are going to die if there is not a sheepdog there to protect you. If you want to be a wolf, you can be one, but the sheepdogs are going to hunt you down and you will never have rest, safety, trust or love. But if you want to be a sheepdog and walk the warrior's path, then you must make a conscious and moral decision every day to dedicate, equip and prepare yourself to thrive in that toxic, corrosive moment when the wolf comes knocking at the door.

For example, many officers carry their weapons in church. They are well concealed in ankle holsters, shoulder holsters or inside-the-belt holsters tucked into the small of their backs. Anytime you go to some form of religious service, there is a very good chance that a police officer in your congregation is carrying. You will never know if there is such an individual in your place of worship, until the wolf appears to slaughter you and your loved ones.

I was training a group of police officers in Texas, and during the break, one officer asked his friend if he carried his weapon in church. The other cop replied, "I will never be caught without my gun in church." I asked why he felt so strongly about this, and he told me about a police officer he knew who was at a church massacre in Ft. Worth, Texas, in 1999. In that incident, a mentally deranged individual came into the church and opened fire, gunning down 14 people. He said that officer believed he could have saved every life that day if he had been carrying his gun. His own son was shot, and all he could do was throw himself on the boy's body and wait to die. That cop looked me in the eye and said, "Do you have any idea how hard it would be to live with yourself after that?"

Some individuals would be horrified if they knew this police officer was carrying a weapon in church. They might call him paranoid and would probably scorn him. Yet these same individuals would be enraged and would call for "heads to roll" if they found out that the airbags in their cars were defective, or that the fire extinguisher and fire sprinklers in their kids' school did not work. They can accept the fact that fires and traffic accidents can happen and that there must be safeguards against them. Their only response to the wolf, though, is denial, and all too often their response to the sheepdog is scorn and disdain. But the sheepdog quietly asks himself, "Do you have any idea how hard it would be to live with yourself if your loved ones were attacked and killed, and you had to stand there helplessly because you were unprepared for that day?"

The warrior must cleanse denial from his thinking. Coach Bob Lindsey, a renowned law enforcement trainer, says that warriors must practice "when/then" thinking, not "if/when." Instead of saying, "If it happens then I will take action," the warrior says, "When it happens then I will be ready."

It is denial that turns people into sheep. Sheep are psychologically destroyed by combat because their only defense is denial, which is counterproductive and destructive, resulting in fear, helplessness and horror when the wolf shows up.

Denial kills you twice. It kills you once, at your moment of truth when you are not physically prepared: You didn't bring your gun; you didn't train. Your only defense was wishful thinking. Hope is not a strategy. Denial kills you a second time because even if you do physically survive, you are psychologically shattered by fear, helplessness, horror and shame at your moment of truth.

Chuck Yeager, the famous test pilot and first man to fly faster than the speed of sound, says that he knew he could die. There was no denial for him. He did not allow himself the luxury of denial. This acceptance of reality can cause fear, but it is a healthy, controlled fear that will keep you alive:

> "I was always afraid of dying. Always. It was my fear that made me learn everything I could about my airplane and my emergency equipment, and kept me flying respectful of my machine and always alert in the cockpit."
>
> — Brigadier General Chuck Yeager, "Yeager, An Autobiography"

Gavin de Becker puts it like this in Fear Less, his superb post-9/11 book, which should be required reading for anyone trying to come to terms with our current world situation: "..denial can be seductive, but it has an insidious side effect. For all the peace of mind deniers think they get by saying it isn't so, the fall they take when faced with new violence is all the more unsettling. Denial is a save-now-pay-later scheme, a contract written entirely in small print, for in the long run, the denying person knows the truth on some level."

And so the warrior must strive to confront denial in all aspects of his life, and prepare himself for the day when evil comes.

If you are a warrior who is legally authorized to carry a weapon and you step outside without that weapon, then you become a sheep, pretending that the bad man will not come today. No one can be "on" 24/7 for a lifetime. Everyone needs down time. But if you are authorized to carry a weapon, and you walk outside without it, just take a deep breath, and say this to yourself... "Baa."

This business of being a sheep or a sheepdog is not a yes-no dichotomy. It is not an all-or-nothing, either-or choice. It is a matter of degrees, a continuum. On one end is an abject, head-in-the-grass sheep and on the other end is the ultimate warrior. Few people exist completely on one end or the other. Most of us live somewhere in between. Since 9-11 almost everyone in America took a step up that continuum, away from denial. The sheep took a few steps toward accepting and appreciating their warriors, and the warriors started taking their job more seriously. The degree to which you move up that continuum, away from sheephood and denial, is the degree to which you and your loved ones will survive, physically and psychologically at your moment of truth.

Lt. Col Dave Grossman is an internationally recognized scholar, trainer, and speaker, who has authored or co-authored numerous books, including On Combat, On Killing, Stop Teaching Our Kids To Kill, and Warrior Mindset. He is a founder of the Warrior Science Group and Killology Research Group, and trains police departments around the nation, as well as the FBI, Homeland Security, and American and foreign special operations groups.

THANK YOU

Thank you for taking the time to read my book. If you enjoyed it, please take the time to add an honest review where you bought this book. While this book was a labor of love, I want to thank several people, without whom I would not have been able to do this:

- God. Thank You for placing me where I am, and giving me the gifts and talents that allow me to serve.
- My wife, Christina Donihue. She put up with my long days and longer nights while I researched and wrote this book. She patiently gives me the freedom to work the long hours that I work for the church, and supports my ministry and business ventures.
- My family. They accepted the times that dad spent in his office writing. Thank you, kids.
- My editor, Kathryn Gerard. She made me sound better than I naturally write. Any mistakes in this book are mine alone (usually from ignoring one of

her suggestions).

- My friend, David Cassiday. He was a sounding board, grammar nazi, and cattle prod to get me to finish this book.
- My safety team members, past and present. Their dedication and willingness to serve has been a lift when I've needed it most.
- My church, Frontline Community Church in Grand Rapids, Michigan. They offer a place where grace and healing overwhelm rigidity and rules. Here is an authentic experience with Christ's redemption.
- Bill Abrahamson. As Facilities Manager at Frontline, Bill was not just my direct supervisor. He is also a friend and mentor.
- Pastor Brian Blum. As Senior Pastor at Frontline, Pastor Brian was brave and allowed me to answer a call form God to create a ministry that was unknown. Even when I mess up, he supports our mission and my leadership.

I know that I've forgotten some. If I have not named you here, it is because I'm occasionally an idiot and forget to thank folks. Thank you.

ABOUT THE AUTHOR

Bryan Donihue is the founder of Sheepdog Development and has a long and varied life experience -- most of which has revolved around either safety or working in the church. Currently, he serves his church as the Safety Team Leader, which is a combination of the two.

Bryan is a former Reserve Police Officer in Indiana and has served as a manager at one of the largest security firms in Indianapolis and as an officer at a private university in Indiana.

Bryan is also a partner in a company that offers training and consulting for small and mid-sized business. With his background in teaching and training, Bryan is able to explain concepts and impart knowledge to those who desire it. As a seminar developer and leader, Bryan's seminars on various topics have been successful and well reviewed by the participants.

Prior to his current role in the church, Bryan has served as a youth leader, both as a volunteer and as a youth pastor. In 2008, Bryan approached the senior pastor at his church and discussed forming a safety team in response to growing violence against the church in the United States and around the world. Starting from the ground up, Bryan has worked with community and church leaders, as well as the local sheriff department and their tactical team, to better keep the team's mission: To make the church a Safe And Friendly Environment (SAFE) to encounter God.

The church where Bryan serves is an active church in the community, catering to broken and hurting people. With quarterly outreach events that serve 1500 - 3500 people, the challenges that the Safety Team face can be daunting. Bryan constantly works with church staff and volunteers to help minister and reach people for Christ while providing a safe environment to do so.

Bryan has taken his talents and abilities for speaking and creating public seminars, as well as his gifts in teaching and leading, and he prayerfully decided to create this new business, serving churches and families. Sheepdog Development is the combination of Bryan's passion for God's church and families, his knowledge of safe practices, and his talents in the areas of teaching and coaching.

Sheepdog Development offers training and consulting for churches and their safety team ministries. Sheepdog Development also offers seminars and individual consulting for parents on the topic of internet safety as well as seminars for parents, churches, and child services organizations dealing with the topics of media violence and its effects on children and youth.

Bryan Donihue

What They Don't Tell You About Church Safety is Bryan's first book.

Connect with Bryan online:

Direct E-mail: bryan@sheepdogdev.com

Website and blog: http://SheepdogDev.com

Facebook: http://www.facebook.com/SheepdogDev